Breath
of a
Child

Discover and allow yourself
to be who you were born to be.

Donna M Rinelli

BALBOA.
PRESS
A DIVISION OF HAY HOUSE

Balboa Press books may be ordered through booksellers or by contacting:

Balboa Press
A Division of Hay House
1663 Liberty Drive
Bloomington, IN 47403
www.balboapress.com
1 (877) 407-4847

Because of the dynamic nature of the Internet, any web addresses or links contained in this book may have changed since publication and may no longer be valid. The views expressed in this work are solely those of the author and do not necessarily reflect the views of the publisher, and the publisher hereby disclaims any responsibility for them.

The author of this book does not dispense medical advice or prescribe the use of any technique as a form of treatment for physical, emotional, or medical problems without the advice of a physician, either directly or indirectly. The intent of the author is only to offer information of a general nature to help you in your quest for emotional and spiritual well-being. In the event you use any of the information in this book for yourself, which is your constitutional right, the author and the publisher assume no responsibility for your actions.

Any people depicted in stock imagery provided by Thinkstock are models, and such images are being used for illustrative purposes only.
Certain stock imagery © Thinkstock.

Printed in the United States of America.

ISBN: 978-1-4525-4561-5 (sc)
ISBN: 978-1-4525-4560-8 (e)

Balboa Press rev. date: 8/14/2014

Contents

I dedicate this book
to every living thing on planet
earth. We are souls that dance together
in perfect harmony.

Preface

After many years of being hard on myself feeling as if I was never good enough. I wanted to get rid of the mind chatter that was in my head and the triggers that I had built up in my life. I just always felt in my life as if something inside of me was not happy and got tired of blaming others or other things for being the problem. To tell you the truth I never really knew what was bothering me.

I knew I had anger for my abusers but really could not believe that it had affected me the way it did. But, I invited them into my life now because of the anger I held. I was told that nothing happened to me and how I was making this all up in my head and how by not saying anything was the way to get over it. So I hide it away somewhere in my mind, but it came out in other ways in my life.

I was able to remember my life since the age of two and could see how my path had lead me to where I was in life, and how I prepared myself for my adulthood. Throughout my life I met all kinds of people from many places. This helped me to understand and have a good idea what issues people were having in this fast paced life. Sometimes someone can spend their whole life trying to find who they truly are and I was able to see how there are a lot of ingredients that make up a human being. Some of these ingredients can be a deterrent keeping us from who we really are. As I investigated these ingredients I could see how the ego worked and that we are our soul. In our soul there are the blue prints of who you are and found that we reflect that into the world as humans using love, understanding, and allowing. Along with many other feelings that seem to blind us from a path that could bring much happiness in our life.

As Respiratory Therapist working in a large trauma two hospital and work with many people on life support and comas, and being around many sad situations, I wanted to live a happier life than I had been. To enjoy my life and live it to its fullest. I had seen how life could change in the blink of an eye and how precious it is.

So after raising my children and as I started working my profession of choice, I should have been happy in life. But, I had something inside of me that just was not helping me in my life, so I knew it had to go. I decided to take this journey of self-change and improve how I felt about myself and my world.

Also that it's not what you do for a living or what you have that makes you who you are, but it's your soul helping you to do what you do for a living. It's what you were born to be and if we just allow ourselves to listen to that inner voice that tells us what we really want for ourselves. Then we can hear our path and by doing it with love, helps get rid of all the things that are in the way and can truly help us live a fulfilled life.

I do not write about the actual abuse, but in turn write about how it made me feel throughout my life. I wanted to change and knew that if I lived with this fear, anger, regret, and hate that I would never have the chance to live a better content happy life.

I knew that I could not erase my past, but found it to be more of a tool to use to help others in my life. That once I began to heal, I found my environment to be more supportive. I also noticed how others reacted to me in a more positive way, and how I see my life as safe and a content place to be in. Sure things happen and this is not a perfect world, but what I found was I am able to handle those times in a better light then I had in the past, and not worry if problems was coming.

I wrote this book so that I may help others, and perhaps go away with something that will get the ball rolling. I also write about how I saw life through the eyes of a child and take you back to when I was young. How I can see now from my childhood how my abuse, although bad, helped me to shape the person I am today

Whether you have been abused, have regrets, anger, or hurt we all want to be happy. But, I can tell you from personal experience that happiness is possible, and you can live a more fulfilled life. I was born to be who I am today, and by doing so it has given me happiness. But, now I realize in order to see the world as a supportive place and feel a part of this evolving system, all I had to do was change how I was seeing things. To change my thought pattern, while having patience, giving it time to take form.

I'm Not a Victim Anymore

For years I lived with abuse and even after many years when it was over it kept me a victim for most of my life. I realized that I no longer wanted to feel emotionally handicapped. As I got rid of the baggage it made me feel very good with a sense of wellbeing, helping me to have more room in my life for the things that really mattered. I grew tired of trying to plea my case in so many ways. The triggers and daily thoughts gave me the right to blame others, for things that were happening in my life. As I worked for two years to make changes in my life on the things that were being rejected by me. I wanted to concentrate on the ones who truly wanted to be a part of my life; taking the good with the bad. I wanted people to accept me for being me. As a child I longed for my own family in life and I realize that I had just that. To curse it would be such a waste.

What being a victim meant for me required that I give up the feelings that kept me back from having a happy life and to have the life I so longed for. Being a victim meant to live my life in fear, never getting truly close to people. Being a victim only brought what I so wanted to forget in my life, never letting it go. Like any change it was not easy for me to release these feelings at first. I have always been strong on the outside and I wanted a smooth calm way of being in my life. I wanted a better way of looking at the world, letting go of all the mental abuse that chattered in my head. Was I perfect all the time? No, I would be lying if I said otherwise; I had to see the truth about myself, so that I could see it for what it was. We all have choices in life and I choose to feel loved and believe that I am loved. How you imagine and think becomes your world inside of your mind, creating your own life and the way you see things around you. Why choose a world full of trauma and fear? Think about what it is in your life that needs some emotional change. That was the question I asked myself.

When I decided to stop being a victim from bad situations that happened to me, I knew it was going to take some time and work on my part. I hid so many emotions and it was very hard on me. I felt guilty as if everything that went wrong was my fault. I had a lot of things to sift through getting rid of all the loose ends. So I changed it by making my mind up that I wanted to change. Then I had to focus on what really bothered me and change the way I thought about it. I no longer was looking for anyone's approval, nor was I going to allow anyone to interfere with my peace of mind.

Try not to look at change as such a hard and painful adventure. Look at change as getting what you really want, but realizing it requires some work as well. It simply takes time and means giving up something that you have been doing for quite some time. So, a death needs to occur. Not a death in the sense of the word, but a death within yourself, letting go of something as to never seeing it again. Sometimes letting go of an emotion can be a very difficult thing to do and perhaps that's why we hold on to them for so long. But, I can honestly say that when I decided to truly let go I found an instant relief in my life, as if a weight had been lifted from me.

Sadness seemed to be a big part of my life because of how I was thinking. So, I had to rewire my mind creating better thoughts. I just wanted to be free of this tangled mess that I was allowing myself to be in and the feeling I had placed in my head about myself. I needed to have it out of my life once and for all. I found that it held on to my will. In fact, my whole life I needed to get through all the layers which made me who I had become in life. I have always trusted my intuition, but I wondered if I would be able to untangle all of the emotions that masked my true self. I believed that we have someone in the spirit world watching over us, because of a childhood experience which I will explain later in the book.

We like staying in our comfort zone, but it keeps us from doing new things in our life. I had to break away from that and get out of the crazy cycle. I thought of it as my mind saying no, but making my body do it. I was able to meet new people and start to have calmness in my life. I realized I was getting completely out of control with the energy I was putting out and it needed to be fixed. Many times I did not handle it in a correct way, but it really didn't matter anymore about the abuse and mistakes I had made, as long as I was able to move forward and leaving it behind.

I started to work with peace knowing it would work out as long as I had calmness and patience. I allowed things to come natural and I reached for calmness, quieting my inner knowledge. This helped me to listen for the directions for myself. In order to move forward I had to go through many emotional deaths that I kept alive for way too long, making me feel trapped for many years. Some days it would creep up on me like a bad habit waiting to consume me. I had to change and realize that when we become an adult, we are responsible for how we handle our abuse. We can harm others and ourselves through our actions by staying in a victim's mode, but it does not give us the right to treat others cruel just because we were treated that way in the past. By doing this we start to become bitter and lonely inside. We cannot blame others for our actions. By learning from it we can help to learn to love ourselves as well as others. Throughout this book I will explain how I saw life through the eyes of a child and how I worked through many hurdles helping me to find who I was born to be in life.

Wide Open

I was born November of 1965 during the black out and lived in Westchester, NY. My father built the home we lived in at the age of eight-teen. A long curvy drive way surrounded by trees on each side led to the house. In the back of our house was a wooded area with a small cottage. It was the first home my parents lived in as husband and wife while their first dream home was being built. The cottage was later changed into a guesthouse, for friends and family to stay in whenever they came to visit. Later in life, I was told that Alan Funt was our neighbor during his famous Candid Camera TV show, as well as Jackie Gleason.

My father owned a large plumbing company and we could see it whenever we drove past it on the freeway. There were many white and orange trimmed work trucks which surrounded the building. He had achieved a lot at such a young age becoming very successful. Even though he had help from his father with money, he was able to take on the responsibility running the business. Besides, he learned his plumbing skills with tough love by his father. My father was very particular; knowing everything there was to know about plumbing. Even at the age of two I could remember thinking how amazing my father was and how I was so proud of him. I believe these were happy times in my parents' life.

My older sister who is two years older than I, was a very quiet child compared to me. I was a naturally, intuitive, curious, and a living nightmare of a child. That led to quite a ruckus in our household. My mother said I was a screamer and seemed to be my father's favorite. It could have been because of the curly black hair and dark green eyes, which was given to me from my father. I never considered myself to be like my father and always wondered what made him tick. The closeness was more towards my mother and sister. In fact, my mother called me misses, "me too," because everything my sister wanted to do I followed. I had looked at it as a proud younger sister wanting to be a part of her older sister and feel my mom may have seen it as jealousy. However, I suppose it was her way of pushing me to be an individual and it was her calling to help me to do just that. Like most children sickness seems to come with growing.

I always seemed to wake up in the middle of the night and many times I would listen to the sound of the darkness, listening to all the things you would not hear during the day, such as the ticking of the clock in the living room or the house settling into the ground. I guess you could say I was nocturnal by nature. This made my mother crazy; as I am sure she lost much sleep at night due to me. I always seemed to get into one thing or another giving me the nickname Seek and Destroy. A name my Grandfather got from the show Lost in Space and the name fit me perfectly. But, as a child I could not understand it because to me I really didn't mean to get into everything. I was just a very curious child.

As children do they seem to find boxes more fun instead of the toys they came in, so many times my father would bring me a cardboard box home. I would place it on the head of my bed, put it on its side, and insert my pillow into it. Then I would put my head on my pillow that sat in the box as I slept at night. This may sound funny, but I enjoyed it very much. I would have a hard time falling asleep most nights and counting sheep did not seem to work. That could have been because I really didn't count very well because of my age, but mostly due to lack of patience. However, at times I found my own way of falling asleep pretending I was swinging back and forth on a swing. This helped me to fall deeper and deeper into sleep as I felt the rhythmic mantra. Many nights I could see the sandman reaching over me with his sack and sprinkling magical dust in my eyes. The crust you get in the corner of your eyes in the morning called eye boogers, to me was the dust he had placed in my eyes the night before.

Surrounded By Life

Although, my father built and provided a home for us he was rarely home, due to his business. His cologne would permeate the air throughout our house, showing signs of his presence. What a big responsibility for a twenty two year old especially during the sixties. With all of the urges that generation had embedded in them to make changes.

My bedroom was separate from everyone else and sat next to the kitchen. In the front of my room was the living room and I always knew who came in and out. I had used my bedroom wall as if an artist would use his canvas. The walls in my room had different color crayon marks and drawings all over them. A bad habit I had at that age and a habit my mother hated. After many times repainting my room she finally gave up and I was free to express myself on my bedroom walls. Although this was gross, I had a booger collection on my wall in a small area of my room. There I collected them and drew a big green circle around them. Now that I look back, it was no wonder I was born to be a respiratory therapist. Mucous and secretions are a major part of our line of work.

Puff and Stuff was my favorite show and I loved singing Popeye the Sailor Man. Winnie the Pooh, by far, was my favorite character and I loved the way he made honey look so delicious. I wished I could join in whenever he would put his paw in the honey pot and pig out on the gooey golden sticky sweet syrup.

On one particular day I got my wish and found my mother's honey in the kitchen. I was so surprised to see the honey bottle in the shape of a teddy bear and would have preferred to have had a big honey pot instead.

There in my bedroom closet I sat and took the little yellow cap off the long skinny cone like top and bit a piece of the plastic top off to create a hole. Then I sucked all the honey out and squeezed the bottle until I had eaten every last drop, leaving no trace of my crime. Later I regretted it and never had the urge to do that again, as I can still feel it in the back of my throat to this day, but the love I have for honey and Winnie the Pooh will always remain.

Due to my parent's young age; they loved to listen to the most popular music of those times, such as Jimi Hendrix, The Beatles, and Bob Dylan. Most night's music continually played on low throughout the night from their turn table. I loved the holidays and can remember actually seeing Santa flying in the sky with Rudolph and his red nose glowing with the moon shining very bright. My imagination was very clear as to what I wanted to create in my world as a child. I loved spending time with family. Grandma and Grandpa always made the holidays Rockwell picture perfect.

Easter was so special with fancy dresses and Easter egg hunts. Family made themselves at home, so everything seemed laid back and calm. Christmas was so exiting and the humor my grandfather had, kept my endorphins on an incline at all times. I did not know until the age of forty, but I seemed to be my Grandfathers favorite.

He was a joyful five foot little guy, mostly bald headed with some gray hair that started at his ear and went around his head and the top was bald. Now a day they call it a runway. He would joke about his haircuts and ask if he looked different. His skin was a very fair complexion and he wore black framed glasses with a large Italian nose. He had just the right softness to give a great hug. So, spending any time with him was great, but the holidays seemed to make it much more special.

Once he had me wrap a set of tools he had bought for himself and had me address it to himself from Santa. It really was a secret joke between my grandmother and him, as I am sure he took some extra money once again for more tools, because being a mechanic was his life and joy. His specialty was VW's and was the reason my mother bought one later in life. It gave us such a chuckle after seeing the look on my Grandmother's face. It gave us many years of a great story to tell around the dinner table. Their home had such a good feel to it, which left such an impression on me throughout my whole life. This was a place where I found love, joy, and peace. I guess you could say that it was the catalyst that kept me reaching for a family of my own throughout my life and helping me through my pain.

My grandparent's home was white with black trim that sat on a small hill, with a bay window that stuck out on the front of the house. My Grandmother always kept three electric candles lit in each section of the window. She would turn them on in the evening time and they glowed in the window until late at night. In front of the bay window was a narrow concrete walkway with flowers on each side that led to four concrete steps that sat to the right of the bay windows. Black decorative designed metal railings were attached to each side of the steps that lead to the front door, surrounded by a small patio. It was covered with a white metal canopy on top that draped like a curtain in the front. To the left of the door was a black mailbox that hung from the wall, but the back yard was where we spent most of our time.

The driveway that was on the other side of the house led to the back yard and was where my Grandfather parked his white VW bug. On the whole side of the house, under the window in a flower bed he grew cherry tomatoes that permeated the air. You could not help from stopping and picking some of the earthy, sweet tasting fruit before proceeding to the back yard. The bulk of his garden was tucked away in the very back on top of a slope. The slope made their backyard a great place to slide down on a snow sleigh in the winter. Sometimes we would slide all the way to their back door step.

His garden was surrounded by a mesh fence that ran horizontal in the shape of a rectangle, which ran from one end of the back yard to the other. My Grandfather's garden was beautiful and this was the reason for my love of vegetables to this day. I can feel my Grandfather in my own vegetable garden today in which I owe his great skills to the beautiful vegetables I grow. My most joyful memory was the cherry tree. I would sit for hours picking and eating cherries. I loved to talk to the birds as I looked through the trees with the sun peeking through the leaves. I always had cherry juice all over my once clean shirt, because of the fresh dark red juice that squirted out as I would take a bit of nature's sweet candy. To this day, I still adore cherries.

The patio was a great meeting place. On really hot days grandma would sit and relax while smoking her cigarettes and enjoyed a nice cold glass of

TAB. Evergreen trees surrounded the patio and the smell reminded me of Christmas. The metal canopies kept it nice and cool in the summer. Many afternoons I would fall asleep on one of the plastic green leaf designed cover lounge chairs and I can still remember the smell of the plastic as a musty weathering smell.

I loved the sound of their house at night too and loved the feeling of the carpet underneath my feet. The sound of the refrigerator was the only sound throughout the house and their home had a unique smell to it. It reminded me of the smell of the delis in New York. My Grandmother was always cooking, so the mixed aromas lingered in the air. Sometimes I notice that smell in my house at times, especially around the holidays.

My grandmother was five foot five with a medium bone structure. Her hair was dark brown the same color as her eyes and she kept it very short with just a small puff to it. The curls were never completely fluffy and as she got older they turned more into pin curls. Her skin was dark complexion with a natural dark reddish tint color to her and she wrinkled very young. I was told that our great, great, grandmother was a princess of the black foot tribe and that our great, great, grandfather was Italian. So my grandmother got her skin I believe from the black foot tribe. So because she had eleven siblings during the depression, it gave her the hard shelled personality she built for herself. But, I have never seen her as happy as when she was with my grandfather. I am sure he kept her laughing all the time and as far as I could see when I was around he did just that. My grandmother was a clean freak and her house was well organized and well kept. I just loved being in every part of that house.

So many wonderful memories I have kept in my mind and heart. I could write a full book on my Grandparents alone and the love they shared with me at that age. However, what was to come would later stay with me throughout my whole life.

Taking A Trip

As I got up in the middle of the night like usual, I would walk around our house until I fell asleep on the couch like so many times before. But, on this one particular night as I climbed out of bed and entered the living room, I expected to see my parents awake and send me back to bed. Or if lucky, I would find them fast asleep in their room, so that it would give me full range to explore the house. However, this night they were in neither place.

At first, I became very scared and began to cry. I wore a red pajama full body jumper with soft plastic soles on the bottom of my feet, which scuffled across the hardwood floor as I walked. I could not understand what was going on. When I checked to see if my older sister was still there, I found her fast asleep in her bed and felt at least I wasn't completely alone. As the tears rain down my face, I began to develop a very stuffy nose and the more I blew my nose the worse it had gotten. I was very confused, calling their names throughout the house and checked again for my parents in their bedroom.

As I entered the attic where our toys were kept and at times my parents allowed people to live there in order to help them out, but on this particular time no one was occupying it, I could see tucked away in the corner on the nightstand, a little container. It had some form of substance in it. I carefully picked up the container and took the top off and pinched some powdery stuff between my fingers. I was careful to only take a very little, as I had seen it done a million times before. When I did see it being done, I would ask what it was for and was told it was for his stuffy nose, but it was only for adults. I then sniffed it in one of my nostrils really hard and the burning sensation was very overbearing, but I was able to keep from spilling the contents in the container on to the floor. In fear that I would have gotten into trouble from getting into something I should have never touched in the first place. I was finally able to put the top on the container and I went back to the living room. From there, everything became very different. What I had taken is still unknown to this day, but I suspect it was why I had the experience I did.

All of a sudden between my parent's room and my room a doorway appeared magically. I felt as if I was in a dream state forgetting about the absence of my parents and my curious imagination caught my attention. I entered what seemed to be the room. The only light in the room came from a long vertical, rectangular widow that sat on the opposite end of the wall and I was viewing it from the doorway. There was no curtain covering the window and it was a really sunny day, but no sunlight was coming through the window, but enough to be able to see inside the room. I remember I could see leaves blowing back and forth as the breeze passed through them and the tree outside the window seemed to come alive. Looking back, I think I was really in my room with the crayon art and the dim light from the living room. In the middle of the room was a large wooden box the size of a large TV. One of the sides was open and it lay on its side, giving me the feeling that it was an invitation to get in. I could see myself in the box curled up in the fetal position. Even though I did not crawl in the box, at times I felt as if I was in the box and other times I felt as if I was outside of the box, but yet looking at the box watching it all happen. I focused my attention to the window; I could see people looking in at me with a croquet mallet in one hand and the wooden ball in the other. Then I could see them all gathering in the yard playing as I flew over them, then quickly returned to the room.

At this point, the box was gone and as I moved my attention further to the right corner of the room, the lighting in the room changed to more of a natural setting and I could feel the temperature change to a cooler climate. Still in a haze I fixated on the sound of the air around me. I then could hear whispers just low enough to where I could not understand what they were saying. Suddenly, I noticed a baby crib in the right hand corner of the room and people looking through the window. In those days I was introduced to so many relatives that I was used to all the new faces. So, even though I did not recognize the people staring in the window, I still felt they were family.

They seemed to be looking at the crib with a large baby in it. Then I suddenly realized the baby in the crib sucking on a bottle was me. I found it very insulting because I was a big girl and drank out of a cup and sleeping in a regular bed. I can remember playing with the nipple from the bottle in my mouth and could feel it as I chewed on it, while it made a squeaky sound. I remember feeling as if I wanted to go outside and play crochet because it was something our family would do during gatherings. The people in the window stared at me as if someone in a hospital would look through the glass at the babies in a nursery. They would wave to me and talk about how good of a baby I was. I felt eager to go outside and I then could hear someone say, "Leave her alone, you will wake the baby," then the scene changed from there.

All I can remember was suddenly being in our dining room, a room I rarely went into, because we ate in the kitchen most of the time. There I sat with my mother and father under the fancy wooden table and the chairs neatly tucked underneath it. My mother sat on the floor under the table to the right of me and my father in front of me. Even though the legs were in the way, we seemed comfortably nestled between them and the legs of the chairs did not seem to get in our way, but felt as if they were a barrier both at the same time.

What we were doing next would seem very funny or gross, however way you choose to see it. We were picking our noses and we actually were measuring our boogers. I guess you could say that boogers brought me to become a Respiratory Therapist, and I guess you could say I started studying my profession at a very early age. We were playing as if we were in a contest to see who had the biggest one. My mother was the winner and I believed it was due to her large Italian nose that resembled my grandfathers. Next, what happened stayed with me throughout my life and think because it happened to me at such an early age, it's what has made me very spiritual through-out my life.

I found myself in the living room in front of the couch. The couch was snuggled in front of the TV with much of the living room behind it. The living room reminded me of my missing parents giving me an over whelming feeling of fear. Behind the couch was a very bright light and sweat poured down my face because of the extreme brightness. The light seemed to make me feel a bit nervous and can recall an overwhelming feeling that gave me such anxiety. As the bright light came from behind the couch and seemed to be so bright that I could not see past it. I could see the light in the middle get brighter, projecting long thin beams of light around it. From nowhere sitting on the couch in front of me was my other grandmother, who my father and I resembled. Although the light was bright it suddenly stopped and turned into an illuminating glow. A tall image of a woman in white appeared with long bright glowing wings that hung on her back and the edges were fluffy; giving the wings a soft look. She had her hands together and had long beautiful brown hair that flowed in the air around her, in slow motion and she had a hazy mist around her. Her face was like a thin sheet of glowing light and I could only see her dark eyebrows never seeing her face.

It felt so real and at this time my grandmother was teaching me about guardian angels and how they would protect me. She explained that everyone has one and if it wasn't for my divine intervention at the age of two, I felt I would of simply wondered out of the house. I found out later that my parents were in the guest house with friend's playing cards. For many years, on occasion, I had nightmares and my mind seemed to be opened more to the spiritual world. It was not until I had my daughter that I started really believing in reincarnation.

Even though it was daytime my mother had the kitchen light on and she had Julia Child on the TV. Her show made my mother chuckle loudly at times. I couldn't understand what made her laugh and when I asked her what was so funny; she would say that, "Julia was the funniest cook ever." On this one particular day, I assume it was spring because all the windows were open in the house and the curtains danced as the wind blew. The smell of lemon, fish, and spices filled the house. My mother learned her great cooking skills from my grandmother. We ate the flavorful fish for lunch together, as we sat on a bench in the living room. She fed me from her fork off the tin foil that she had cooked the fish on, laying it on a plate. I sat wiggling around talking away and one thing I said to her later was so profound to me later in life. "I was once your mommy and now you're my mommy." I can remember how strongly I felt about it. I never mentioned it to anyone afraid of how silly it would sound, but I never forgot about it, so I kept it to myself. Until I had my daughter then it really connected more with me.

My daughter has always from the time she could walk, buttoned up my shirts, and adjusted my skirts. She seemed very motherly to me and to this day she has the need to feed and clothe me, so I get pieces of clothing throughout the year from her. As a toddler she loved to sit on my lap and play with my black long curls. On this one day she turned to me and said, "I use to be your mommy, now you're my mommy." That to me was not just coincidence and explained to me the mothering I received from my two-year-old daughter. I really felt God that day.

Once I had my son Chad I experienced a connection of strength that helped me to see my own strength as a person. He's a reflection of my thought pattern and I have noticed how he listens very carefully to me. So I had to be very careful to show him things he would need to use in his own life for his soul. So with each child it has helped me to grow as well and the connection I have with each one of them is one of a deep soul connection, one that we have shared perhaps in many lives.

Though my father's business flourished with much money he seemed to be going through his own thing in those days. He lost everything he had worked hard to build and went bankrupt. At the age of five my mother packed up my sister and I in her new blue VW Bug and headed to Province Town, Massachusetts. My mother bought the VW bug after the so-called divorce settlement.

The Land of Province Town

Province town is a picture perfect harbor setting with a long narrow red brick antique road. Rainbow shops, restaurants, and stores sit between each side of the road. The Hare Krishna had a place off from the road and would mediate in their front yard daily. I learned so much about meditation by watching them in amazement. Many times I would sit on the steps at the rainbow shops and the owners would give me crayons and a small coloring book, with rainbow pictures in it. I would color, while at times the owner would play the guitar and sing. I can remember missing my father, but was used to his absents. I adapted very well. I was able to run wild in those days at the age of five. To my amazement after I had my own children, I realized how young I was to be running the streets; but that's how it was in this small cozy town. Plus, freedom was part of my world, and I could feel it in the air. I was able to go and play in the morning, as long as I was back before dark. The beach was my favorite place to be and I do not remember the water being blue, but its dark sandy color gave it a gentle feel. Many times the smell of fish would permeate the air in the morning, and then dissipated by the late afternoon. I had a pop belly and freckles with short curly brown hair. The brown hair was from the long afternoons in the sun and in fact, I got the name Watermelon Belly from camp one summer. The girl who gave it to me meant to make fun of me, but I laughed and saw the humor. Therefore, I guess you could say I continued the name by telling the story, making me very popular during summer camp and felt I was liked very much. I loved to make people laugh even to this day which was a gift given to me from my grandfather.

I made money selling the daily newspaper and they were so thin that I could carry twenty at a time. The roller skates in those days were almost all metal. In fact, I would say that they were ninety five percent metal. You had to wear your shoes to use them; by placing your foot onto the shoe shaped metal sole and sliding it back and forth to adjust them to fit, then locking it with a metal key so that it would stay in place. The back heel had a two inch plate that sat horizontally in the shape of a half circle. Even the part where you placed your front toes was metal and after you were done they looked like some kind of a robotic sandal on wheels. If you have not figured it out yet, they were one size fits all. We wore the key on a string around our necks and it seemed to be the style back then. I would make pennies on each newspaper purchase and always made enough to buy a piece of pizza at the local pizza shop next door or other things I wanted. Once I saved up to buy the newest product a mood ring and a pet rock. This could be the reason why I love natural stones to this day and you will barely see me without one around my neck.

The Pinch a Penny candy store was like walking into a candy factory. If the smell did not drive you to this delectable sweet nose candy then all the colors would. In 1970 you could get a lot of candy for ten cents. It is no wonder I had such a watermelon belly. The army surplus store was set up with a green army canopy and I can remember the newness of items. The store had a very distinctive smell only to be described as if you were camping and sleeping in a tent. It was during the Vietnam War and the store had all kinds of army products and my favorite was the sun tan lotion. It came in a thin metal canister in the shape that snuff comes in today. The store clerk told me it was the actual lotion they used to protect themselves from the sun in the army. It did not smell like sun tan lotion and had a very waxy smell to it, but found it was very good for mosquitoes. Therefore, whenever I ran out of suntan lotion I would return with my quarter and buy some more.

The pier was much fun especially during the summer. I met many different types of people and helped many visitors find their way around the town. Of course, I was the good host and would recommended many places. Once, I can remember getting on an old wooden ship that could have been the spitting image of the Mayflower. I walked right on the ship with the tourist, and went for a full day of adventure. At one point, the ship stopped letting everyone jump off and go swimming. I can remember getting worried that I would not get back before dark and would worry my mother. I believe I was mistaken for someone's child when I got on the ship.

Many times I would swim with the other local children. The tourist would throw coins off the pier and we would compete to get it by swimming and catching it, before it was lost on the bottom of the ocean floor. I never did really well, but the older children would help me get some money at times because some of the tourist would say, "This is for the little one." There was some kind of a verse we would say to get the tourists to throw money to us, but I cannot remember it. We would hold the money in our cheeks, so we would not lose it while swimming, pretty stupid now that I look back.

The town crier was my best friend and dressed like a pilgrim. He wore black shoes with a long tongue sticking out, a long doublet with long puffy sleeves and extremely large square collar, with a black pair of pants and white stockings. He wore a black belt around his waist and a long black steeple hat. It was a perfect pilgrim costume. He ran through the street saying "Hear Ye, Hear Ye, and shout the time of the hour, while ringing his large hand held bell. He also went around helping the tourists with information. When my friends and I would sell lemonade we would give him one and he gladly welcomed it on those hot summer days.

Tuna fish was my favorite food and I always rushed home to watch dragnet while I ate my mother's cold tuna fish sandwich. I seemed to crave the taste of fish as if becoming part of my surroundings. I loved chewing on dry salted cod and really enjoyed the fishy taste. Many times I would watch the fishing boats come back to the harbor, with large amounts of tuna and could not believe how big they really were. My mother was friends with the Harbor Master's daughter and they would have lobster parties so much my mother got sick of eating it. So, it wasn't unusual for a metal tub to be in our kitchen full of large lobsters. Sometimes one would try to get away and break free from the ties crawling out of the tub. Of course I would go screaming throughout the house and my mother would capture it and put it back in the tub. It was cruel to me then and it's cruel to me now, although I must say I have eaten much lobster in my life.

I would often go on the reefs, way out in the ocean and collect starfish and silver dollars. Then dry out the silver dollars and sell them to tourists, but throwing the starfish back.

Many days I spent visiting the public museum and it became one of my favorite places. Pilgrims Tower sat in the back and is a brick sandstone tower in the shape of a lighthouse, but with a crown around the top. I would sit on Plymouth Rock near the entrance of the tower while eating my lunch that I had prepared that morning for myself. This was before they decided to place the rock into a glass cage because of the tourists, chipping away at it for souvenirs.

I taught myself how to ride my own bicycle back in those days, but in the most unusual way. We lived on a hill and our house sat right in the middle of it evenly. At the bottom of the hill was a little mom and pop small wooden convenience store and running horizontally was the red brick road. Thank goodness that there was very little traffic around then, when I decided to do this, or I was just very lucky. At first I would try to ride down the hill at full force balancing naturally and as soon as I felt that I was getting close to the end of the hill, I would jump off and there the bike would go right into the store. Most of the time the bike would go on the side of the store and stop in the grass, but there were many times when it hit the store. I don't know how many times I must have gotten in trouble with the store clerk, but as soon as it got to the point that they threatened me with talking to my mother, I had already learned how to ride a bike pretty well. I loved all the colors, air, ocean, and other things that came with this beautiful town. I will always remember this place as a great memory that holds so much joy in my life.

Let the Games Begin

My mother had met someone and at a drop of a hat she was married. This, I would say, is the shift in my life when I learned about the real world. Until now, I have realized that not only did it make me stronger; it made me who I am today. Because we moved a lot it was hard to establish a sense of home in those days for me. Church was something I did on my own and looked forward to, so that I could get away from the madness and away from everything. In those days church would pick you up right at your front door and I went to so many different churches by the time I was ten; I had a well understanding of how others viewed God. That is how I was able to remain open and respect others opinions on their own spirituality and beliefs. I knew at the age of eight that I was pretty much on my own on this one. The secrets I had to keep, were my abusers way of controlling me

When we left Province Town it was very heartbreaking for me, because of all the sudden changes. Honestly, I really don't think my mother had the energy to see what was going on with me, because of how good I was at masking it and keeping it deep inside of me. I tell my mother to this day that she should not feel guilt what so ever, because she was not the abusers. She should not pay for others bad karma and it was their choices, their karma.

We moved to Fort Lauderdale, Florida into a very small two room efficiency on the second floor. In the front was a living area and a small kitchen tucked in the back. A door to the right went to the next room which was a bedroom and on the left, as you walked in was a bathroom. I felt unsafe and unsettled I saw how the world was not an easy place to be and felt that was why I began going to church on my own; it was a place to be treated with love. One day while getting off of the school bus, for the first time in my life I experienced a traumatic horrifying experience.

As I started walking home with a group of children, I noticed a beautiful yellow lab puppy with a very nice collar around his neck that jingled as he started running toward us. In the distance down the road I could see a car driving a bit fast. The puppy was running towards us wagging its tail. His collar tags clanged together and what looked to be a smile on his face. We tried to yell for the little fellow and the unthinkable happened. The puppy ran right in front of the moving car. He was completely run over from the front tires to the back and then rolled a couple of times in the air. At this point the owner came out of her house screaming and I ran straight home crying all the way there. I could not take much more and really felt that I needed to talk to someone about it, but knew it was not going to be possible, so I kept it in. That night I had the worst nightmare ever because it was so freaky to me and I felt it was my fault. The guilt of not saving that precious animal weighed very heavy on me. I woke up crying and remember walking back and forth as I wrung my hands together. I went to the door that was locked on the other side. I was in and out of sleep; I thought I heard noises around me. My nightmare had just begun when the door was answered and I was not understood. This made me feel very lonely and heart broken in disbelief of what happened. I had nowhere to turn to express my feelings and it was only left to go deep down inside of me, creating my pile of more baggage I would carry for years.

We eventually moved to an apartment complex which gave us more room; two bedrooms, a living room, kitchen, bathroom and a small back yard. Many times the neighbors next door would have sugar cane growing through the fence and we would chew on a small piece all day. The bark was so sweet and creamy it was almost addictive. We would suck all of the juice out of the long strains of thread like pieces, spiting it out whenever we were done. I had such thick bushy curly hair and my mother liked me to keep it short. She still would prefer me to have short hair, but that's a thing we have between us that we fuss with one another to this day.

Because we were very poor I received a free haircut in order to save money. There I sat while he cut and chopped at my hair and I could see the long curls drop to the floor. The man who cut it was laughing the whole time as he cut it unevenly and the whole area of my head was chopped to pieces. It was too short to fix, so after the humor he said it was over and I was left to go to school with this awful hairdo.

I woke the next day to my first day of a new school. I was determined to cover it up and all I had was a crochet winter hat with a long tail and a pom pom ball on the end. In order to blend in with the hat, I thought I would wear a red wool winter coat that I had for many years. Once in the classroom I did not blend in with the rest of the children in the classroom and was asked by my teacher to take off the heavy coat and hat. Because we lived in Florida, I'm sure it looked very funny and very ridiculous to the teacher. So having no choice, I finally took off the hat and laughter filled the classroom. When the teacher saw my hair, she looked shocked and understood why I wanted to keep it on. This was during, what I call a bubble test and it created test anxiety which stayed with me until college. It was not until I moved to Big Stone Gap, VA that I had a big respect for nature and the beauty it held.

Growing Strong

I call these days my lumber jack years and that was when I learned about mountain life. The day we arrived I can recall the tall mountains and the misty blue film that covered the Blue Ridge from a distance. As we drove right into the mountains, we drove around what seemed to be in circles. It was like a spiral staircase as we climbed, giving it the illusion that we were not going anywhere. The first thing I can remember was the beautiful wild, pink, and red roses that covered the sides of the mountains. The smell of roses permeated the air and if you were to pick them up the pedals would fall off, as if water was running through your fingers.

The higher we went, the more the air pressure felt as if my head was going to explode, then my ears would suddenly pop and the pressure would release. I really suffered from a migraine that day and it was so bad that I could not see past the large spots in my view of vision. I had bad headaches before, but this was the worst I ever had and to this day I have not experienced one like it since. We were never able to join any clubs, have friends over, go to sleepovers, or even go over to other people's homes. Because of my outgoing personality, I only socialized when I was at school. I found as an adult that there were many activities in the town and there was much history there, but I never knew they even existed.

Our home was the last house on a long stretch of road. The house snuggled in the corner away from everything and it was like an old white smaller version of a farmhouse. It sat evenly on an inclined mountain. Our front yard was like being in the middle of a hill, giving our yard a slant and at the bottom of our yard was a cliff. Below it was a rail road track and the train would go through on schedule every morning and evening. We did not have heating built in to our house except for fireplaces we used in the winter. We would cut trees from the mountain, leaving us no time on the weekends to rest from school. I handled so much wood between cutting it and continually feeding the fires around the clock, that the dirt settled under my skin and it was hard to get it completely washed off. I was in very good shape at that age of thirteen, four foot eleven weighing ninety nine pounds and I can honestly say it was all muscle. The guys who came to get wood and help called me Crusher, because I did what I had to do, because in reality I wanted to get done. I became very good at chopping wood and learned how to do it with one arm using an ax. Now I am lucky to get half way through a piece of wood using both arms without feeling like it's time for a nap.

Even though the evil rang through in my life, I found much peace in that mountain. Many hours I would spend hiking, knowing every part of it. I would literally have to hang on to the thin, what I called paper trees, so that I could climb to the top.

Fresh mountain water was pumped into our home and was one of my favorite places in the mountain. There was a pathway that lead to the reservoir and was made by other people's footprints from constantly stepping on the earth, making it a nice bald natural path to walk on. Each side was surrounded by trees and dark green forest. The area had a huge square deep concrete reservoir surrounded by earth and it was buried so deep into the ground it gave me the willies. If you were to fall into it there was no way out, so I made sure I stayed very clear of it. This is where the water was collected, giving us running water in our home. It was the attraction of the mountain, because past the reservoir sat a small babbling brook that ran down stream. In the middle was a large gray boulder rock, flat on the top and perfect for sitting on. Many times I would sit quietly, close my eyes, and listen to the water that flowed downstream, while it passed below me. Just being surrounded with nature gave me a feeling of being safe. I felt as if I belonged there and it brought a new meaning in my life for me. I felt that God was very close to me there, feeling as if I was not alone. I found kindness in those mountains and I spent all the time I could there.

My dog Bosco was very special to me because it was the only dog that we were able to keep. I did not like that he could never come in the house even during the winter months and it really bothered me. Once Bosco contracted a case of the mange and his medicine was motor oil poured all over his body, then he was left on his runner in the snow during the winter's months. It worked but I felt so sorry for him. The only contact the dog had was when I took him on my walks through the mountains. We spent many days together hiking and escaped from reality. It was the only thing that kept me sane during such trying times.

One summer at the age of thirteen I joined a summer program and worked at the public library. I was very surprised to see that I was able to join the program. I learned much about how a library was run. Due to my love of the great outdoors, I volunteered myself to do some of the yard work, so that it would save money for the county. Plus, I really liked the manager and could see how she really wanted to do a good job, so I agreed to do it.

I cleared all of the vines with my friend who also was on the summer program. I was determined to remove all of the vines that made its home around the huge oak tree. I grabbed large armfuls of the dark green vines and blindly made my way to the huge pile I created, as I carried them up and down a slight hill. As I pulled all the weeds from the large tree I covered myself with them in my arms. After the work was done, I was so proud of the job I had accomplished and the praise we received that day felt good. If I only knew then that in the evening it would turn into a nightmare.

That evening when I took a bath I noticed a very irritating itch that continued to spread all over my body. I tried to put a cool towel on me to relieve some of the inching, but with no luck it just seemed to make it worse. Weeks later, when I returned to work, the supervisor of the summer program came into the library to find out why I had missed so much work. He could see what the problem was and took me immediately to the doctors. There I found out that I had a severe case of poison oak. I was very surprised to see such a reaction from the supervisor and doctor, because weeks before I was in much worse shape.

During those weeks I suffered tremendously. Poison oak surrounded every part of my body. My Face was so swollen I looked disfigured and this is no exaggeration. I went through a bottle of ivy dry a day and was so consumed with constant itching I was beside myself. Now that respiratory is my specialty; I realized why the doctor was so upset to hear what I had gone through. He told me I should have come in to the emergency room immediately. Knowing what I know now, I could have easily died from my trachea closing off; from the inflammation keeping me from getting any air. When I say it was everywhere, I mean it was everywhere including my throat and private parts. My fingers were so large I could not even bend them. I itch just talking about it. But, with the grace of God, I recovered and the medicine the doctor gave me helped it to completely dry up.

While driving in the company van back to the library, after visiting the doctor, I noticed my family driving by in the car. I was so excited to see them and what a coincidence to run right into them, I proceeded to wave in excitement and could see everyone laugh and wave back.

When I came home from the end of the day, I walked in the house to greet everyone. I was laughed at and made fun of. I was considered a hypochondriac, that I was so happy to be going to the doctors. So, it was the joke of the family. I felt as if I was the only one around when I suffered from my poison oak. I mean, couldn't they see how much suffering I went through? This put me through so much stress of not being believed; it stayed with me through- out most of my life.

Sickness was something I was used to dealing with by myself. I knew that a doctor's appointment wasn't possible and checkups were never. I wondered how I was able to deal with infections without antibiotics and realized that maybe this was why I have such a good immune system today.

One particular sickness lasted for a month. During those days, I threw up regularly and because it was never ending most of time I threw up bile. I now wondered how I was able to keep from dehydrating. I lost weight very quickly and was very skinny. I was pretty close to skin and bones, but I began to feel better and was able to build my strength up.

There was a place in the hallway that a chair was placed and it was used for my punishment. I would have to sit there for weeks, only getting up to go to the bathroom, meals, sleep, school, and to clean the kitchen. Little did he know that I strengthened my mind all those days and much of my time was spent meditating.

All I wanted was to be understood and feel as if I belonged somewhere. Whenever I felt something, I was told that it wasn't how I felt. So I was confused about how I felt about my emotions most of the time. I never completely understood my feelings for many years.

There were other times I was severely sick, to the point where I needed immediate treatment. Severe cuts were always taped up and left to heal on their own. The exposure of illnesses children encounter and come in contact with can wreak havoc on ones respiratory system. Many times I would go through a lot of rolls of toilet paper to spit in, because it was too painful to swallow. I suffered with ear infections to the point that I would have blood that would trickle out at times. To this day I have a lot of scar tissue in my inner ear, but I must say I never get ear infections anymore. If one was born to work a job with lots of exposure to many diseases, then it might be a good idea to get molded and groomed, so one can fight the kinds of exposure that you could get in a hospital.

I gave my mother all of my savings from my summer job, so that she could get a divorce. She was ready to leave and I so wanted us to leave too. Therefore, we traveled in our VW bug to Florida and moved in with my grandmother.

After a year my mother got her own place in the next city from where my grandmother lived. There I spent my teen-age life and met some wonderful people that would be in my life to this day. Some passed away and some still living. We moved there when I was fifteen years old. It was the best time of my life with many friends, but I had so many issues and insecurities I was unable to have a normal relationship. In the eighties and living thirty minutes from Daytona Beach Florida, it was not hard to get caught up in all of the events such as: Bike week, spring break, race week and so many other events that take place there. I lived with my mother and other siblings, for three years and there was much peace in those days. This too was a great time in my life.

When I look back time seemed to slow down in those days and what was four years felt like a decade. Around nineteen to twenty two it seemed as if I was pregnant the whole time and that was when I had my children Faith and Chad. Years later my children grew up and I was settled in my career. I thought of the many obstacles I overcame, but I began to hear all the garbage that was settled in my mind. I wanted to get rid of it. Simply for the fact that I was aware of it and second it gave me a very lonely feeling. One thing was for sure that having my children in my life helped me to change cycles and patterns that needed to be stopped. Now I look at my children and see such strong wonderful human beings and by allowing them to be who they are is the only job left for me to do. I could be there when they needed me to help with advice and they could take it or leave it. So, I knew when everything became quiet, I had to do something with all of the chattering that was left over that I had ignored for so long.

Nitty Grtty

Years later I found myself with two adult children and a husband I have been with for twenty two years. After fighting my way through college with two small children, I became a Respiratory Therapist helping and healing others. Yep, life should be nice and peaceful, right?

Well, have you heard the roof cave in with windows shattering in the background yet? I must say after the merry go round stopped, I could hear in my mind all of the things I thought I let go, came back like a nightmare. I was so consumed with raising children, running a house hold, and going to school. I really didn't see all the anger, hurt, and frustration I had inside of me.

All the abuse, the feeling of being alone in my life, and feeling like no one loved me was going to destroy me. I felt as if I would do better on my own and the wheels turned and turned in my head. The more I festered on it the more anger I was creating in my life. I was more upset that the people who hurt me would not say they were sorry. I wanted them to fall to their knees crying for mercy saying, "Please, please, forgive me for all the pain I caused you." Well, that was never going to happen. Besides, did I really want to dig up a can of worms? I looked at my life and seen what it was that was important to me. One thing was my peace of mind and the other was the love I had for my own family. I didn't want to create a scene and dig up all of the pain, so I had to find a gentle way of approaching it.

Once I was able to see all of the baggage in my mind, I took my thoughts to the next step. First, I refused to let myself go to the place that dragged me down in my thoughts. It was those negative thoughts that were keeping me in a position of sad situations, allowing them to linger in my mind and inviting my surroundings to be less than desirable.

I found myself getting angry at my mind for allowing myself to think such negative thoughts to the point that my world looked very bleak. I began to feel as if I had been hoodwinked by my thoughts causing me to drown in sadness. That is when I decided to take control of my thoughts. I started to tell myself that I had no time or room in my life to worry about such mundane things and that I refused to think negative thoughts. Now I know this is not a perfect world and things were going to happen. I was no longer going to worry about things that consumed my thoughts and life to the point that I could not live in the now. How dare such thoughts even enter my mind and I began to look at it as an uninvited guest that insisted on being rude. After a while, I began to increase the percentage of good thoughts in my mind, replacing any bad thoughts with true positive ones. This is when your growth begins to shift in your life, increasing your vibrations in the universe. We are all working with energy in our life that fit our vibrations. As human beings we use energy to create what we want in life. We attract it and change its vibrations as growth continues.

So what do we do with others who we feel are not keeping up with our growth? Maybe later in life they decide to go back to school and start a career at a late age and you decided to do it earlier in your life. Does this make you more advanced in life than them? Or maybe school is not their choice in life and they want to become a fisherman out in the open wide ocean. To me whatever we choose in life to do is our profession no matter which one you pick. This is how we keep our world going and just like a watch cannot work alone without some of its parts, so it is true as humans and our world, we have evolved and chose to live.

If you have a lover, child, or friend that is not where you think they should be in life, just remember that we all work on different levels throughout our life. The ego at times wants us to feel as if we are better than someone else, so we get blinded by any advancement others may be having, for what is right for some people may not be right for others. The same goes for others who are being patient with your growth. If someone is not on your level of thinking just simply be kind to them and help that person instead of criticizing them. To want someone to be jealous of you is the egos way of wanting us to feel as if we need approval and to be jealous of someone is the egos way of wanting us to feel as if we are not good enough. I needed to find a way to make peace with my abusers and toxic people in my life without being bitter.

So how do we love those who are toxic in our life without allowing them to harm us? It's very simple, love them. Just because you love someone doesn't mean you have to have dinner with them every night and talk to them on a daily basis. There are other ways you can love without keeping yourself in harm's way. With love for others we can accomplish a reflection of love back to us. I was once told by someone close to me, that people do not change and found later in life how lonely it must be to see others in that way.

People change minute to minute, day to day, and thought to thought. An overheard conversation can change a life. The earth is changing all the time, a constant flow of ecosystem that thrives on change. Like it or not we are a part of that system. If we can understand that then it will help our life to flow better. We stunt our growth by believing in one way only. These were thoughts that ran through my mind and wanted to take the road to least resistance, allowing myself to see the world in more positive way. There were so many situations in my life that I have thought of as misfortunes, but I have been able to see them as lessons throughout my journey.

I wanted to learn how to rewire my brain create better thoughts, changing how I felt. Once I had the knowledge that I could rewire my brain, I was able to understand that I had full control of my life and everything up until now I created, like it or not. That by having this control I was able to create what I wanted, but there was a catch. I had to create what I wanted and it had to be who I really was inside. Be the person I was born to be. Just like that child who loves repairing their stuffed animals and dressing up in a lab jacket with a stethoscope around their neck, then grew up to be a Respiratory Therapist, but I had others things about myself beside my profession and I wanted to find them.

Although you may have a profession that you have always wanted as a child, there are more things involved with being who you are. So I had to reach for it, learning new information that has been there since I was born. From the time we are born to the time we die and perhaps in the afterlife we will be forever changing.

When my children grew up, I had to grasp the concept that I had to find other things in my life to help me grow. I had to go through and understand many things about myself and I went through many changes. To get what we want means some work on our part. Change can be overwhelming at times, but with each step one can make it to the place where they feel comfortable and safe.

Ugly Anger

I don't want to make it sound as if my changes came so easy and that all my days were sunshine and rainbows. The truth is I had some sad and cold days. I never let it be seen from people who I didn't know very well, leaving my family to see my sad pain I carried around with me. I never knew when those days were coming. Even though it was hard to go through, afterward I felt as if I had learned something from it at the same time. But, I no longer wanted to go through those moments in my life any more. I wanted to feel free from it.

When I turned eighteen I found out little by little how bad it was. There were days I didn't know if my feelings were right or wrong. Oh, yes I knew the basics, but when it came to my feelings I never knew if I handled situations right and I questioned everything about my feelings. That was the way I had looked at it most of my life. It was a way for my abusers to keep the dirty truth from coming out. It was a way of making me feel confused and responsible for their behavior. Whenever I spoke up I was looked at like a liar and confused person. I never let go of God in my life and always tried to treat others with kindness. I hated it whenever I felt as if I was hurting someone's feelings or someone was being hurt.

I had days that I screamed at the top of my lungs behind closed doors and cursed what had happened to me. Many times I was mad at myself for not seeing it sooner. I felt guilty and shame within myself. Some days I spent so much of my energy with these out bursts of hurt and anger, I would feel as if I was dehydrated because I cried so much. When those days came they lasted for hours and the rest of the day I spent sleeping, because I had worked myself up so much to the feeling of exhaustion.

Any time you are hard wired to think the thoughts you do from your childhood it takes a while. You should not feel so guilty for taking those steps backwards, or feel you blew it because you went into your old bad habits. It takes constant perseverance and not giving up. Keep standing up dusting yourself off. It's like you are trying to cross a road determined to get to the other side. As you walk you are stepping in pot holes, but you continue and learn to walk around the pot holes. Even though you fall and trip you keep proceeding forward and eventually you get to the other side safe. I felt as I got older that it was good for me to get it out, but I didn't want that anymore. I felt a relief as I did, but it never went away. So that told me it wasn't working. That is why I wanted to reach out and help others. I wanted to help others connect to peace and help clear the cob webs, so that the path is much clearer to see. Most of all I wanted it for myself as well.

As humans we basically learn as we go through life, we simply are not born with all the information. Therefore, we need learning tools to get the information. Once we have those tools it's up to us as to what we do with them. However, once we have the tools we are then able to fix the problems. We must see the light and the truth about it, so that we can move forward in a positive direction. Many times we do not understand our troubles, but we may have to start digging around the dirt to find it.

Sometimes just ignoring it is not the answer and especially if you are having problems adjusting to it. Sometimes we do not see that these feelings are even bothering us. We may think we are doing fine and have been able to get past it. That is fine when many times we have worked through those issues and we are able to adapt. One question I believe must be answered. How happy are you in life? Are you finding that you are going through some anger issue, or having those dark days that I was having? Are you reaching your full potential and allowing yourself to be who you truly are? Is frustration a regular emotion for you?

Anger is like carrying a bag of dirt around for years; it has no use, doesn't look very pretty, and only weighs us down. Although you may think it keeps you safe, in reality you begin to look like a bitter person to others and cause pain around you. If you do not get rid of the anger you begin to take the job of being an abuser in some way, or allowing the abuser to enter into your life.

When you first got abused I'm sure you never wanted to be like that person and anger has no use in your life or body. We have to be responsible for our own actions no matter how hurt we were in the past. When we start to understand the abuse we then can understand our actions. By not doing anything about our actions at this point makes us very responsible for the lives we affect.

We can look at it as a two headed sword. One side we can use as a tool, or the other side we can use as a destructive weapon. Many times we may feel stuck in this life as if being happy is so far out of our reach, but really it's so close. Just because we fail at times going back to our miserable habits, only means to get back on the bus and don't give up. Take that ride and begin to enjoy it.

Make a promise to yourself to live your life at this moment with much love, giving you a gift to live the life you so much want to have. You only punish yourself by keeping love so far away. Therefore, use what you have today and move forward without being harsh on yourself. Today is a new day, new time, with many new events in the future, so live in the now, for now.

Get rid of the pollution in your mind of bad thoughts and what happened in the past. Continue to reach for new memories with new thoughts combined much love for yourself and others. You don't have to continue to be bothered by using your childhood as an old memory or crutch. Use it for the building blocks to reach out to yourself as well as others. I also had to live with the choices I made in my life up till now. Some good and some not so well, but I had to bless it all.

Find what emotion that seems to seep out to the outside world and needs some improvement in your life. It was funny that I could feel the anger but not love. Why was I picking anger in the first place? I felt that I was never good enough, feeling different from others. So I put up a wall that kept me safe. Sometimes we feel as if we cannot confront our pain. Sometimes we don't get the chance to be face to face with our abuser, because of many reasons and it doesn't matter because the abuser is so sick they do not see that what they did was wrong. If they did you might have gotten an apology and perhaps it would have not happened in the first place. So when we are left with that pain we are left with what to do with it, causing sadness and perhaps passing on that pain to others. I had to get to a place of feeling safe in the world knowing that it is all behind me. I knew I had to change my thinking pattern. Louise Hay has a great book called "You can Heal Your Life," which has continually helped me very much in my life. She teaches about affirmations and the power of words and thoughts.

The day I realized how my numbness affected my life was the day I let the wall down and began to feel. I think I cried on and off for about a couple of weeks. There were many times I cried very loudly in my car when I was alone. In reality I was healing from my pain and actually feeling it for the first time in my life. I allowed it to take its course without the anger.

Numbness felt as if everything in my body had stopped, as if the air flow was stagnant around me. When I opened up my heart and mind to love, I was able to breathe better and felt a sense of calmness in my life. I felt as if I had been gone for years somewhere else and started to see the truth for what it finally was. I began to feel like I was living in the world and finally being a part of it. I hated how I handled things, but felt as if I could not stop it. I was addicted to my anger and I understood that I was creating the world I was living in, holding on to that anger. I was only hurting myself because the world I was seeing in my mind was only being seen by me.

When I went through the abuse I formed my numbness there so that I could not feel. This way I could become separate from the abuse and able to live through it. I had to learn to feel again and open up channels in my body that had been dormant for years. Getting over it was like going through a death and it really felt as if someone had died.

Triggers are those awful actions that set us off, due to some past problem. It could be just how someone treats you in line at a yogurt shop to suddenly begin to get frustrated easily. It could be misunderstood by you, from someone just saying or doing something innocently to you and mistaking it for something bad. This creates the domino effect and before you know it you start blaming others for how you are feeling. What comes out may be some deep-seated issue.

As humans we have the inner need to bring others along on our own personal journey. That is why they call it a personal journey. I did not want to say I was happy, I wanted to feel it. If you find that this is hard for you, try to think of your mind as a computer panel and what is programmed in is what comes out. Therefore, the next time I came across a situation I replaced it with a good thought or action helping me to change that trigger. After doing it I looked at it as rewiring my mind creating new connections. There is a good movie out, called "What the Bleep Do We Know," and explains how we are actually addicted to our emotions, due to things called peptides that are released when an emotion is programmed. Basically it's like having any addiction and you crave more of it. So, being mindful of your surrounding can help to think healthier thoughts. Meditation is a great way to help focus on your environment creating a good ambiance. I found after a while good habits started to form easily and it became automatic.

Imagine if you could clean your brain out of all the bad thoughts and replace them with good memories. To rebuild your mind and create new links, creating new neurons and new electrical pathways to better thoughts. Pain has a lot to do with anger and I found that when I became hurt, anger was a way to protect myself. Whenever I felt hurt I would make sure that anger was not a part of it. This took some getting used to, because for years I used this tactic so I would not feel hurt. As I worked with my pain I found this to be one of the biggest challenges and most of the time the anger was just stuffed down deep inside of me. I wanted to become quiet inside of myself and learn to look at things before I reacted.

The last time it happened I swore that it would never happen again. I had to accept the fact that it was nothing that anyone could do for me; it was that I had some hidden problem that needed to be free. I found that my emotions became very raw once I decided to change, as if a flood gate had been opened.

I had acted as if it never happened to me and I could see how confused I was on those days that it surfaced to the top. I hated to bring it up again having to deal with it, but in turn I was keeping it alive through my anger. But, I knew I needed to do this and finally give it a resting place. But at the same time it was hurting me inside and I needed to rid myself of this destruction that was killing me slowly.

One day I had met a young man who told me about his childhood and how he was abused. Full of tattoos some carried his pain, with pictures of negativity and anger on his skin. He told me how he had to raise himself and how he didn't have any family. My heart felt for him. I could see the destruction that he had put on his body and mind. He had a very strong exterior with a hard personality. I could see how his anger was affecting his world on the outside and most of all I could see how his anger was protecting him. He made it very clear to everyone he met that he was not going to be hurt again. He really felt he was a good person and that he was okay with others as long as no one messed with him. I thought to myself that to me this sounded very unsafe for someone to be around; because of the unknown anger he carried. What was it that would set him off and trigger him to get angry was the question? After talking with him for about twenty minutes, I thought of what I could say that just might spark an interest in him. Perhaps that could maybe change his life and help him. I knew that I could not change his complete thinking pattern, but perhaps I could say something to encourage him to take another path. I told him I bet that he was very artistic. It wasn't his tattoos that made me feel that way; I just felt this about him. All of a sudden you could see a glow in his eyes and he began to tell me much about his talent. By the time I left him he gave me two thumbs up with a big smile on his face.

I still say a special prayer for him often. Sometimes it just takes a little understanding and a little respect, with a few kind words, that could change someone's life forever. You just never know when your words will affect people. Even though you may never see someone again your prayers and love mixed with kindness will help your heart to open up to others in the world.

Should we feel guilty in our lives when it comes to living the life we so desire? Should we feel guilty because someone tells us that they believe we should live a certain way? A true life is filled with a person's individual dreams of who they truly are. You leave behind and carry with you a legacy of the people you have touched. The ones you helped along the way, some are known to you, while others are in the back ground, because of your presence, persuaded them to create a good deed. There, it grew like an ivy vine in a garden spreading to others.

Spectacular things happen when someone begins to heal or has healed. A light shines more in their eyes; they begin to have calmness around them and things flow much easier in their life. This was true for me when I let go. Once I released my anger, I began to have a feeling of freedom.

Painful Denial

Denial is something that keeps us from learning and advancing. When you hurt someone and never admit it to yourself or pretend that nothing happened at all, it's called denial. How can we learn from these things, if we simply act as if they never happened? I'm sure it makes us feel as if we are protecting ourselves by denying it, but when we do this we are doing a big disservice to ourselves and simply cannot fix that which is not discovered.

Denial comes in many forms, but all add up to stunting our growth. Really look at yourself without being so hard on yourself. Face and feel what it is that you are so afraid of. It may not be as painful as you thought. Think of it as a new journey of much growth and learning. It's a foundation to build and create new and better habits. Once the denial is no longer denial it becomes acceptance and with it comes new doors and new opportunities.

With everything changing around us and the fast-paced life that we are living in, we have to remember to have patience and to enjoy each gift it brings to us. Because I kept being a victim for so many years, simply due to not letting go (knowing I could easily use that card again), I had to watch out not to fall back into those nasty habits. But, once I practiced good thought patterns rewiring my mind, I was able to diminish my bad habits.

I hid my abuse thinking that I had no right to feel anything and that I was wrong for feeling the way I did. This clouded my mind and I questioned everything I felt. I wanted someone to love me my whole life unconditionally and the pain blinded me from the love that was right in front of me in the mirror, and to now look at the loving people in my life.

Denial hurts the ones you love. Once you have accepted it after you have looked at it, it's times to move on to the lesson of acceptance. I found with denial, it just gave me an unsettled feeling like something was not right. The hurt was heavy on my heart like eating a big piece of raw dough that just sat in my stomach. I reminded myself on those rough days to love the feeling acceptance brought. The feeling gave me one of heading for the finishing line. I could see it in a distance and knew that there was a light at the end of the tunnel, because I created that light all by myself. I did not have to depend on others to light my candle for me anymore. I had my own matches.

Now there are many ways and different things in life that can keep us in denial. The denial of a very sick loved one happens very often and I see this in my field. Perhaps it's not denial and is faith. To me, until someone completely passes, I don't blame a loved one for holding on and it's not for me to judge how they handle it. It's not my moment, I am there to help heal and take care of their loved ones, and that is it. Everything else is up to the family. We don't know what their true wishes are more than the family does. They were there in early stages of their loved ones life. There were talks around the dinner table of how they felt and thought about death.

You don't want to wait for your growth just because you are waiting for someone to admit their denial. Do yourself that big favor. If it is someone that is still a part of your life, then use love and kindness in all of your actions. This will benefit you more and help the situation and relationship to flow better. Through love and no resistance you can accomplish a lot.

Time really does heal us from pain. Unless there is a magical way of wiping it out, we will always remember pain in our life, but it's how we handle and see that pain. We can use pain throughout our life to help others. There are so many foundations built on people who have suffered in the world resulting in helping others. This love helps us to bond together and bring light into our life. Its gives us moments of feeling wonderful, peaceful and loved; when we heal spreading it to others.

The pain we have endured in the past we lived through. Some of us barely escaped and when the survival techniques were no longer needed, it hard wired us to keep it for safekeeping. So what do we do when pain has been so unbearable that we feel as if we cannot go on any longer? We learn to trust again getting rid of the need to punish someone else for our pain, which creates more pain in our life.

It's hard when one is hard wired in their mind to have to deal with such trauma. Many times when I see people who are addicted to drug or alcohol I don't see them as bad people. I see them as a hurt person who never was able to get over some kind of pain in their life. They may have denial in their life, masking it with drugs. My heart goes out to those people, because they do not know that they hold the key to a better way of life. Although I feel for them, they must know that they are responsible for themselves now and that if they want true happiness they must take the first step in recovering. To admit to it and refuse denial, seeing it for what it really is.

Children suffer much pain in life because of adults who feel they have the right to be a victim. Adults need to look at the way things have changed in their life and the responsibility they now have. We do not want to become that abuser and breaking the cycle is very important to do in life, so that all can heal around you. Sometimes the pain is so unbearable that we don't recognize it for what it is. We deny that pain and it comes out in other ways. To make peace and move on is one thing, but to ignore it and not move on is another thing. We really need to make peace with it, so that the triggers and bad thoughts do not cloud our mind.

To make peace with oneself we must deal with all these emotions we tucked away long ago and perhaps this is why we don't deal with them in the first place. If you have an ache in your heart due to some loved one, who has passed or from something that has happened to you, which has caused such sadness in your heart. When things happen in one's life such as losing someone in life or death we have a tendency at times to get angry denying we are hurt.

There are many stages to getting over death, but in my own opinion we all handle it differently. I drove myself crazy trying to figure out what stage I was in and how come I wasn't in the stages listed in order. Then I realized that I was going through my own thing here. As soon as I got rid of that thinking I was able to relax into it. We are constantly going through stages in our life. From the time we were born we are changing daily. Not just physically, but internally as well and we project on the outside the kind of light we have on the inside. Sometimes we are, our own enemy. So denial only hurts oneself, by allowing one's self the freedom to be able to work through the changes, giving the feeling of recovery.

Changing Ocean, Shifting Waves

I had the need to want to change others around me and this was a very hard for me to learn. I felt like most abused children as if I could control my surroundings. I knew something needed to change, but I denied that it was how I was feeling inside that needed the real change.

We can help others and it can help change something in their life for the better, but we cannot demand that someone change. It has to come from them and we can help by acceptance. Once that happens then it gives others the feeling of freedom to make changes for themselves. If change does not happen and we feel it's affecting our life in a negative way. We simply accept it or move on, but staying around ordering change in someone's life only creates friction and unhappiness.

As you can imagine trying to constantly change the people you love the most not only causes friction, but takes away the love that was seen in the beginning. In my opinion we seem to get bored with people once the bubble bursts and reality kicks in. We tend to get used to things and not be able to see the beauty that brought us there in the first place. Once the newness fades, we stop seeing the greatness. It's like a beautiful view from your window. After a while it begins to just fade in your life and it doesn't get noticed as much, forgetting how you really enjoyed it in the first place.

My children have always pushed to be individuals and they have proceeded to continue to make decisions for themselves. This helped me to realize that through letting them find their own individuality, they were able to think and blossom into wonderful people.

I had to not let my ego get in the way of my vision. It really did not make sense to me anymore to continue to put so much stress in my life. We can be teachers and students, but in this lesson of the world we must learn on our own time giving us free will.

We have a thing called the brain; every one of us sees the world different. Not only are we an array of color and looks on the outside, we are gatherers of truth on the inside. We all learn differently and even though we live together with our families, we all go separate ways throughout the day. Although we may see the same thing at the same exact time, we all have a different experience with other thoughts. It is just as complex as the universe that we are entangled and a part of.

If you have found that you have caused pain in your life, trying to control and change someone, try allowing in gentleness; stop thinking of your growth as if it were in jeopardy. To say someone is keeping you from it, only puts you in denial. Say that you want to get in shape and exercise and you find you are not doing it. You proceed to make excuses about your exercising and you have no time for it. It's only a thirty minute workout, but yet you have no time, finding yourself watching TV for an hour. When you talk to someone about it, you make the excuse that you are too busy with other things and spending time with your loved ones. So we make excuses for the things we desire for ourselves and at times blame others for our change issues. If you make the decision to keep someone around in your life don't complain. Unless you are in an abusive relationship and you are in denial needing others help.

How can we feel as if we own someone in life? I mean we can have them as employees, friends, children, or a spouse, but that gives us no right to feel as if we own that person. When we feel as if we own someone, we then begin to feel we can do with them whatever we please. Try owning your own life, seeing what it is that really sparks your interest. Allow others to live their life with you. This will help you to hear your soul and attract like-minded souls that are ready to learn and want to teach you. It will take you to greater heights and help you to become a loving person on the inside. Every great step leads you closer to what is needed for you right now.

Create good memories in your life. If you have found that you have created bad memories or have been encased in bad memories, plant new seeds and create a new garden of electrical neurons filled and connected to good memories. Start right now after you put this book down for the night, day, or evening. Plan or do something that will create memories. Do something for someone, not just for their pleasure, but for your pleasure as well. Plan something special for your family and friends. Start a new tradition creating new memories in your life.

Life doesn't have to be so painful or feared. Now that you are on this earth, use your time wisely by doing it with love. Never stop even if your baby steps need to go back a foot or two, just keep walking, and continuing through your time in life. For a while in my life I felt as if I was in a batters cage, dodging baseballs shooting out of a pitching machine all the time. Things I found to be helpful in my relationships were the things I looked at about myself very closely. I didn't want to pick my battles, nor did I want to go to war. I have learned; the best way possible to help, is to let it work out for itself, by allowing.

When we are in a relationship we may feel as if we are seeing the world through the same looking glass. Not true, we are not and just like anything we see things different and go to different places. We form different relationships together and we share stories of life with one another. Neither one owns the other, because we are individuals who have fallen deeply in love with one another and choose to be with that person, sharing ourselves with one another. When I was able to make a habit out of listening and stop controlling everything around me, I was able to learn from it and it made things go much smoother than it had in the past. It's so easy to just end a relationship on the basis that your beliefs are different than the others. We all have lived different experiences and in fact, we are different from each other.

To be an individual you have to understand that in a relationship you must have room for your own separate lives. This means feeling safe in your relationship. I have a very close male friend and there were times when he would pick me up and give me a ride to work. Not once was my husband or his wife jealous that we were actually going to be alone with one another and that it was a set up for ruining our relationships. My husband trusts me and understands that my friendship with my male friend was very important in my life. To keep someone from their path only causes pain on your part, leaving you to be consumed with thoughts that really don't even deserve to be recognized. This will give you time to explore who you are, knowing that someone in the world loves you very deeply.

When I began to change the things in my life about myself that made me so unhappy, something wonderful started to happen. People in my life started to radiate more with love and things flowed so much easier. Just like everything in life, change is a constant factor in the world we live in. Although many people can adjust to change very well, some have a harder time dealing with it. One thing we all have in common is the kind of change that takes place in our life we particularly do not care for. Because the world is constantly changing and everything around us never really stays the same, we must all accept the changes that are out of our control. Look back in your own life and see how you once were and how you lived. Your hair, body, and lifestyle were different. Just like when we were a toddler, then teenager, and then to a young adult. Our lives thrive on change in order to teach us. Without change we would not have growth and without growth, we would not exist.

Sometimes the ego can make us worry about mundane things in life and worry so much about our material things in the world, we forget about the soul. We mistake material things for happiness and if we ever lose them or get them taken away we lose ourselves.

So in a sense you could say that once I concentrated on my growth, I began to open new doors and begin new things in my life that I thought were impossible. It made me more relaxed and much more easygoing. It gave me a freedom to be me and I was able to better understand what I needed right now in my life. This helped others to join in and grow with me.

Enjoyable Existence

There are so many ways to live life with enjoyment. Does it mean you have to have a lot of money? Does it mean you have to be popular? What is it that makes us feel contentment in life? Do you wake feeling good about your day, or do you wake feeling sad? So, in order to answer these questions for myself, I removed the ego to find the answer. Did I need money in order to live the life I so wanted? To have or want prosperity should not come with guilt, it's okay to want prosperity in life. To let go of the ego is when you sink into your life with calmness. Not worrying about what others may think and what others may have.

When I started to think of thoughts that get me upset or unhappy and I stop myself from thinking them; by telling myself that I will not allow these thoughts to grow like a vine giving them power to ruin my day. I don't allow my thoughts to get out of hand and I change it around. You would be surprised how fast it works. I find that I forget that I was even in that mood in the first place.

There are days when I would get depressed, sad, melancholy, and other kinds of emotions, but I started looking at them as just what they are and stopped analyzing them. I then could see that these kinds of days would pass. We are very sensitive to what is going on in our environment and at times we allow it to change how we feel.

We all have a dark side and sometimes we hide it from the world and if not confronted in a healthy way, we could get into trouble taking us off our path.

Think of your feelings like a chart. We go through life most the time feeling in the middle. At times it fluctuates up and down depending on the joy or sadness we may be having. It could spike very high if happy, but during very sad situations it spikes downward. Sometimes we live in the middle giving us a feeling of boredom.

So how was I going to handle the moments on downward days? I had to get rid of the guilt that was being built around my imagination and understand that this was a temporary emotion. On those days I would adjust the way I saw things, even if I kept going back to my stressful thoughts. Also a good nap works wonders when under stress and of course meditation. There are other things that help us in life and that is the people in our life that love us very much. It doesn't really matter who loves you in life whether they are blood or not. All that matters is that you are loved in the world. Surround yourself with them in life. They will accept the new changes in you and you will gather people who will love you along the way. Children and adults find themselves with other people in their life instead of their blood family, due to circumstances that are out of their control. We may be born to a family but sometimes we find love that leads us to another direction. Sometimes as adults, we see in our children the same dream we had when we were young. A dream we perhaps never got to do. Maybe when we are born we are expected to inherit a career from family and expected to follow in their footsteps due to a family business. I can see how people can lose who they truly are in life. We are who we are and that is that. I feel happiness does not exist without being who you are in life. We seem to collect garbage in life; causing bad habits, hang ups and depression.

Let's face it, material things are fun in life we enjoy them. To say you are better than someone just because you have the latest updated computer is just as ridiculous as it sounds. It's okay to feel good about ourselves and enjoy our life with our prosperity. But to feel better than someone else, just because you have material things is just not right. It makes you a different kind of person then another, but it doesn't make you better and aren't we all different anyway because of our experiences and thoughts, but yet we are all connected. If you are wondering how we can be so different but yet be connected, because being connected means we must be all the same. Sound confusing? Think of it as a puzzle, each piece is not the same because they are separate, but together they become the whole puzzle making the big picture. We pass up getting to know someone cool, because we have blocked ourselves from having some great relationships. Imagine what one could learn from such a variety of people. To me if we see people beyond their appearance or status in life, we can see the joy of others company.

Enjoyment really does come by letting go of the ego and feeling free from these things that block us in life. Being human is a combination of many factors: spirit, soul, ego, disease, and environment along with many other things. We have adapted to our environment and created all these factors. As a child I wanted to know more about things spiritually and have had people come into my life at the right time. We accumulate people in our life that love us and care for us. What makes a person special in our life?

An example of special people in life is someone who cares about you and wants to get to know more about you. They learn things about you and let you learn things about them. People who love you don't judge you, but tell you the truth no matter how hard it is to swallow and tell you with much love. We also let them do it and respect the advice. People who love us want the truth from you and trust you with it. There's learning and teaching dance going on with no certain pattern, creating a natural flow.

They are people who love you and perhaps become part of your family. As you both adopt one another or have been born into family. There are all of the emotions there, such as; tears, laughter, anger, and happiness, but you always accept one another. When you love someone you accept them, tolerate them, and of course love them through their troubles. These are the things that make a difference in our life that help us to connect to people. I have met some people in my life that I have loved and I have lost in touch with, but that was a time when we needed one another.

We cannot look back at how we were treated when we were very young by people who treated us badly. We must not expect our loved ones to be perfect and know that everyone has something that may irritate others, but remember we too have those characteristics. In fact, when you are close to someone you will see more of who they truly are, because of the comfort level. When the bubble burst and you realize that you are in reality, then you begin the stages of really getting to know one another. When this happens we feel as if something is wrong with the relationship. When in fact it's just settling in like an old house, giving it its own unique cracks.

Many people sometimes get into a habit of leaving when this happens; never giving it time to really work through what a relationship can grow into. Also being married or in a serious relationships may not be for everyone. Sometimes we go through life just enjoying others. Loved ones should not be toxic and hurt each other's feelings. It doesn't have jealousy when you are living your own life with others. It allows each other to form other relationships and it doesn't become possessive. Your loved ones in the world have other friends and people they love besides you. Fear of losing this person should not be an option. Your relationship should be built on trust. I understand that people have what they call a "best friend," and I have one too. They are people who you feel are more than friends and more like siblings. Someone you felt you knew forever and you might think you lived many years ago in your past life with one another. Friends and loved ones do not play people against you.

Let's look at all the kinds of relationships people have with one another. We connect in so many different ways and some are very short lived with big impacts in our lives. We need one another to help along the way and possibly this love affair we call life is just what our souls need too.

Sometimes we judge to fast and assume things in life that really don't exist. We worry about situations that may not exist, allowing our ego to make us feel insecure. For example: Say that you go to work and you run into a friend. He is a little short and abrupt with you. You begin to talk with him and ask about his day. He has always been very nice to you, but on this day he was very different from normal. He grumbles his words but with much aggravation. You smile ending your conversation and it bothers you most of the day, changing your mood a little into more of a negative attitude. You go home and throughout the evening you can't help but think about the situation, wondering what you had done that was so wrong. What you don't know is very different than what you wasted your time worrying over.

The night before your friend had an argument with his wife and had a very restless sleep because he slept on the couch. Due to a competition he had with his dog over sharing room on such a small space. It left him with a pulled muscle. The next week you run back in to your friend. The first thing you ask is if you did something wrong to him. He looks at you with confusion on his face and he seems to be taken back by your comment as to what you are talking about. He wishes you a great day and smiles patting you on the back.

Can you see how we let things that are not real bothers us sometimes. There are so many examples that I could come up with that could show how we misunderstand situations. To understand this helps us to live without so much drama in our life. So, I always get the facts before I feel someone is lashing out at me, because of something I did. It's so easy to make things up as we go and create a story so big that we tend to miss the whole picture. Just observing the situation before we act is very important and how we handle it is even more important.

The ego wants to keep us confused so that it keeps itself alive. It wants to take over our thinking. It keeps us away from the things that really matter in life. Let's face it unless you see and hear it for yourself don't assume anything. I had to learn this as well in life and find that it helps me to lay back a bit and be the observer. People get very hurt by others assuming something and by judging someone as to what happened really causes much pain. Whenever I judged something I could see how it made me feel inside. The feeling is one of guilt and shame. I knew deep down inside that it wasn't the right thing to do. I have been judged by people in my life and all it did was make me feel bad, as judging them did the same.

We really cannot allow others to bother us when we are judged. All it does is consume you with feelings and thoughts that we don't need. Really when it comes down to it, I really don't care what others may think and assume about me. We all fart and poop and even spit up dark green mucous when we get a respiratory infection. So we have to really stop pretending here. The ego wants nothing more than to make you feel as if you are better than others, disconnecting you from life and keeping you from learning

Just as in marriage there is no perfect marriage, but it's what makes it unique to you and what things we each can tolerate from one another. You will hear couples say that it's a perfect relationship, so for them it is the perfect unique union. So before you begin to judge someone look at the whole picture and remember we are only human here.

As a young child I always saw both sides to things and was told by adults to pick one way or the other. That confused me as a child and always felt I had to choose. I just wanted to be neutral in life and just be. When we are born, we are born with ideas of who we would like to be in the future. Because we have our own energy that helps us to contribute to the world we live in, makes us each unique in our own way. Once we find our uniqueness we then are able to find others with the same interest. Then once we find others, we share our uniqueness on the same shared subject of interest. This is what makes us each different and unique in our own way.

We should look at our own gifts that we were born with and learn to focus and use that energy. I have found for me, meditation has helped me to become more focused on my gifts in life, helping me to quiet my mind. To quiet the mind means to feel content. So when we are content we are able to let things flow better because we are allowing.

So no matter how different people are from our lifestyle. Just remember that by having variety around us in life is what makes life interesting and exciting.

Willpower Required, Support Needed

Before I meet my husband Rich at the age of twenty five, I already had two small children, Faith four and Chad two. I can remember praying to God to help me with raising my children and because I lived in a very tiny travel trailer I wanted more for them. At the time I was working as a waitress with no benefits and when I didn't work there was no money coming in for that day. With two small children it was hard not to miss work due to illness, especially when they would get the flu one right after the other. Sometimes the flu would last for a week. Then I met Rich, we met at the same place we both worked at. We connected instantly and have been together for twenty two years now.

During those times I originally was going to become a Registered Nurse, but I graduated as a Respiratory Therapist when my children entered into their teens. When I entered into the program I never intended to become a therapist, but with guidance I was able to find something that fit me. The nursing program had a two year waiting list. So therefore, I applied for the respiratory program which still had a one year waiting list, but I figured I would give it a shot. I was surprised after I received a call the very next day. I was accepted and started classes two months later. What is really amazing is most Respiratory Therapists really never intended to become a therapist, but found themselves into the program for some reason or another and working in this profession. This may be due to the fact that it's a very young profession and was started around the seventies.

Although, this job was made for me I never thought how much it was going to change me. Working with the sick was not only very rewarding, it was mentally tiring at times. But what I found out was there must be a balance when it came to heartfelt feelings and the ability to back off. The hospital I work at is a very large hospital and covers many areas of health care.

Being on the trauma team I got much exposure to many sad and stressful situations. Much of my time is spent with family and the love I have for my garden with many other hobbies. This helped me to relax in a healthy way. The one thing that really makes me feel good is helping others and the feeling I get when doing it.

I have never felt so much at home as to when I met my peers. I felt that we had much in common and I was able to connect to many people. Was my career stress free? No, but I was groomed to be a strong person. One thing that you learn in this kind of environment is if you have a problem with someone it better get fixed really fast, because there is no room for personal problems during a critical situation. Also, if you don't work it out it better not show its ugly face during it either. I must say that in a critical situation you become very humbled. There is no room for that ugly evil ego and in order to work in that kind of setting you learn that really quick. I learned to be very independent and self reliant person and soft at the same time.

As a respiratory therapist I work very closely to people on ventilators, some know it as life support. I have seen many comas and the hardest part about my profession is how hard it is to see the family mourn a loved one. As a therapist where I work you rarely get to see people recover fully, because they go to rehab or other facilities to go to the next step in their treatment. We prepare them for that next step and make sure that their body is strong enough to continue. So you really have a big respect for life and how gentle it really is, because of how it can change in a blink of an eye. Once it changes their life, it shifts the whole family and each and every one who cares about that individual walks away learning something from the experience. I have become very good at reading peoples lips, because of the lack of ability patients have to communicate while on a ventilator because of a tube in their trachea. Many times when weaning a person off the ventilator sedation must be removed, in order for a person to regain their ability to breathe on their own.

One way I have learned to connect to my patients is to look at them as someone. I visualize each one as someone I know, reminding me of that person. This is how I keep myself in check when caring for them. This was one way I learned to help others giving the best care possible and not lose focus as to where I stand in life.

When a trauma is called overhead the trauma team gathers in the trauma room. Each person sets up their area to prepare for the arrival of the patient. There usually is a very short period of time where everyone is waiting for the arrival. Much talk is happening and anticipation can be felt in the room, but as soon as the patent arrives everyone systematically performs their profession, like perfect team work blending into a perfect flow.

After a while you become a little paranoid doing things in the outside world, because you see a lot of freak accidents. One thing I know for sure is every one of us will be a patient one day. That kind of fate each one of us will never escape from.

When someone is on a ventilator and in a coma, I know they can feel my presence just by the movement of their eyelids, when I enter the room. Many times I have had people grab my hand and I hold it for as long as I can in order to comfort them. Being on a ventilator can be very scary. Imagine having a tube placed in your throat and tape around your month to hold it in place, having someone operating a machine in order to pump air into your lungs. It is not any easier or less scary for the patient and letting them know you care means a lot. I see the instant relief from patients on ventilators as soon as you let them know you are there for them. Their muscles relax and they slip back into a deeper relaxing sleep. So just by spending a short period of time holding someone's hand or talking to them can help the patient to feel as if no one has forgotten them. Some people may think they cannot hear us, but they say your hearing is the last to go.

I have learned so much about humans and how they think just by talking to my patients when being on the floors. Because I work in all areas of the hospital I get my time on the floors. Which gives me time to talk with the patients, while they are there for a short periods of time. I'm able to have wonderful conversations with them and learn a lot about their lives. I have met many seniors who have lived some wonderful lives and seen many things. I take care of many strong veterans of all ages who have had years of illness because they defended our country. Some have lived hard lives while others have spent most of their life helping others. It gives me a great feeling and an appreciation for our men who defended our country. I really feel that most of our seniors feel left out of life because how we view our elders in this country. They are the wise the crones of the world and should be respected as such. It's such a beautiful thing when you see the family of an elder gather in a patient's room. The atmosphere gets changed and you can feel the air transform to a very clear and airy feeling in the room, because of the family who are creating such a loving surrounding. There's a deep connection that can be felt though out the room. One only a history can bring.

When there is a tragic event in someone, life and it affects the whole family, we as care givers know how hard it is on the family. Many times family member may feel their loved one slipping away. Nothing changed me more than when I entered into this field. I see it with new graduates. How, after a while, it changes them and in fact I can see when it happens. They lose their innocence and now see life in a different way. One of the things I like is when the family puts a photo of the patient on the wall in their room enjoying life. When a patient is in a coma on a ventilator they do not look their normal self. So having these photos in the room is a way for the patient to speak saying, "Yes I am a really human, with a real life." Although I connect to my patients, to me it helps me to bond to them in a totally different way.

When my husband became a patient, because of a near death experience, I tried my best to make the caregivers feel appreciated. Every day he was in the hospital I would bath him and change his bed. It really helped him to feel my love for him when I took care of him. Plus it was a big help to the nurses. If you are going to be taking care of your loved one at home and as long as it's okay, I suggest jumping in when you can. I find that when the family is involved with their loved ones care, the patient heals better. I really feel that when we show our family members how much we care for them, they enjoy life more no matter what spiritual plain they may be on and how sick they may feel. When I walk into a patient's room quietly, I make sure to let them know what I am going to be doing, even when people are in a coma. I could not imagine hearing everything that is going on around me and no one telling me what is going to happen to me. They know that there is a presence and you never know when one of them is having a very soulful experience.

I believe during death and near death experiences someone can have an outer body experience during severe trauma. I never ask a patient, but love it when they share one of their own spiritual experiences with me. When you take care of people in the health care you cannot judge anyone. Each person is to be treated the same, no matter how poor, how rich, or what they have done to someone else. I have learned so much about life from the people I work with and it helped me during those times when I felt down.

I'm sure as human beings we all have things that we need to work on. We need to bring better things into our life that does not feed the ego, but things that feed our soul. Sometimes things that we do in our life may not be good for our soul. These are the things that make us hear that little voice in the back of our head saying, "This is not good!" Even though we do these things to get instant gratification, they do not last and is the brains ways of telling us that maybe we should try something else and the souls way of saying, "You can connect to the divine without resistance with much ease." We spend lots of time as humans trying to feel this instant gratification. In the world we don't give natural highs much credit and at times think it's not cool, or how nerdy, but actually natural highs are ten times better.

So this comes to my next subject. Self-discipline and willpower and how it affects us. What are they all about and how come they are so hard at times to do? What's involved in these two things that keep us stuck in bad habits? While physically they are time consuming, it can be hard to get rid of the scratch that is itching at us to do them again.

Self-discipline after a while changes into better habits and becomes natural. Because we are making healthier choices and rewiring our brain to better habits, we change the energy. At times I would feel resistance and a pulling at my will and after looking at it I could see that it was caused from being hard wired from all those years of learned behavior. I had to just say to myself this is going to happen, so find something else to do. Because our brains are hard wired, we have to see that candle in the corner that has a small flame flickering in the background and turning up the light, so that we can see the whole picture. Basically, just make yourself do it and that's that, no ifs, ands, or buts. Let that light enter your life and let it come into that darkness and confront you. See it for what it is and just tell yourself that today is the day and I'm going to do it, now.

I wanted to be more than just worked up about it. What I mean by that is I didn't want to get all worked up about it, feeling my newfound strength only to have it sizzle out within a day or two. When I decided to stop smoking I made my mind up to do it. I was a closet smoker for years and felt very ashamed, due to the fact that I am a Respiratory Therapist. Plus, because I know what smoking can do to the body, I would constantly tell myself that I was killing myself each time I would smoke. I believe in mind over matter, so just telling myself this I felt I was doomed. I was ashamed of smoking and for a couple of years I told myself that I was a nonsmoker. Then the day came, that I said enough was enough and I decided to make some serious changes. I knew that the day was going to come when I had to stop smoking. The freedom I got from quitting really gave me a great feeling of accomplishment.

As the days passed I became much stronger and able to build up more will power with some healthy self-discipline. Also we find the feeling of accomplishment to be a great feeling; this helped me to feel rewarded wanting more. When self -discipline changed to accomplishment it was no longer self- discipline, but a better habit that formed. What about those days when I just didn't feel like dealing with it? This was like a death that had occurred, making me feel very vulnerable. I just wanted to say forget it and I wanted to go back to it. So how I changed those moments was I began a new project such as reading, exercising, and keeping myself busy. One thing I did was begin to drink hot green tea with mint. Whenever I felt a big urge to smoke, I would get my diffuser and make a nice hot cup of tea. Then I was able to drink it giving my hands and mouth something to do. Plus, I was changing my triggers to a better thought. I actually get excited about my cup of tea and look forward to it.

Self- discipline at times may feel as if it's a hindrance and we may want to go back to our old habits, giving us that instant gratification. It doesn't last and all we are left with is feeling bad about it. What we call rebounding and falling hard, because now we are doing the bad habit again and we now feel worse about it. You find yourself giving up this great feeling for the instant gratification again. We can remember how we felt and swore that we would never go back to it again. As we look back later, we remember it reminiscing in our past accomplishment, being hard on our self over and over again. Why do we pick things that make us feel so bad about ourselves later on? It could be something that is deep down inside of us and the reason we picked this instant gratification in the first place.

Willpower is the determination of your strength that changes the allowing to one of achievement. So if you find that you have gone back to your bad habit after many years of accomplishment. Remember those days without being hard on yourself and bring back this new found willpower in your life.

The more we accomplish our goal the better we feel about life and ourselves. If you have a habit that is getting in the way of your family life and it has caused pain. The rewards could be rebuilt relationships. Don't be afraid to reach out to others. Do what you have to do in order to clear a pathway, so that you can easily get through your journey with a feeling of self- worth. There is always going to be bumps in the road.

So if you are in a bad situation and you have these bad habits. What kind of energy are you sharing with others and how does it look on you? Have you ever seen someone transform right in front of your eyes, becoming their new found project of self-change?

Purposeful Imagination

I have found that children are the best at never letting their dreams go. Just think from a very young age, we have been acting out what we want to be when we get older. We amuse ourselves and pretend to be who we want to be and surround ourselves with many projects, loving it to the depths of our soul.

I always understood that just because someone is different does not make them a bad person. That even the quietest person sitting alone can be the coolest person that you might ever know. I never felt I had to be accepted into a group to enhance who I was when I was a child and felt I was the closest to remembering my soul because of the newness of life.

The newest generation that has become adults is the Millennia's. My husband and I have much experience with them, as my two children are part of this generation. I feel that this generation has mastered the art of finding and searching for who they are and they do not care about what others may think about how long it will or has taken them. They love searching and trying new things in life having the courage to move forward.

Most of them were raised by generation X. Don't forget generation X was raised mostly by the baby boomers, who stirred up much of the changes we have today. We told our millennial child how wonderful they were and rewarded them. Dreams are part of this generation and being an individual is much of their plan.

Most of them do not fear the unknown when trying new things in life. If they do fear it, they do not let it become a barrier in their path. Because

I work in such a large hospital, I can spot a millennial a mile away just by the way they carry themselves. They have a lot of respect for themselves. Also don't underestimate them, because they are much stronger than what you may think.

I feel that generation X wanted their little millennial to just feel good about themselves. So if you want some tips on making your dreams come true, just ask a millennial because they have been practicing it all of their life. They have been able to see that with each path they take comes with it many experiences. They collect them like charms on a bracelet. Are they spoiled? Yes perhaps, because they were raised at a time when the economy was good and the energy in the world was different. They are the last generation to know what it is like to be without cell phones, computers, and GPS. To own a beeper in the days my children were growing up was a very expensive device to have. Besides you had to find a phone to answer the call. Cell phones were not around and if you needed to do a project, a trip to the library was needed. I can hear them now, "When I was a child, there were no such thing as the internet in the home." We need the millennia's now to brighten up the next generation that they are raising. I fear that the new generation is feeling the energy of the world, getting bits of information of how everyone is feeling doomed. Especially, with all this talk about the end of the world. So everything will balance out and come full circle.

Dreams are very important in life and they are what build many wonderful accomplishments. It attracts things we want in life and gives us a way to fantasize. Before you get angry at your child for not doing what you want them to do, as far as picking a career that you feel is right for them. Look at your adult child and ask yourself if they are a good person. This should be the part that is most important to you in your life. To stress your child out because they are not who you want them to be, can cause much pain in your adult child's life. There are so many people in the world who do wonderful things just by being who they are and not what others want them to be. We have our children from birth and as parents we have to raise them the best way we can. To give advice, support, and be a shoulder to cry on, but we do not own their life.

The child who loves bugs just may one day become an anthropologist as an adult. Or just like my booger collection as a child and how I grew up to be a Respiratory Therapist. So allow your child to dream letting them try new things. Just not the piano lessons you wanted them to take. Perhaps letting them spend their hour studying and playing with sea shells that have intrigued them for years, encouraging them along the way.

What is normal? We are so caught up on what is supposed to be normal, we get stuck in the same old routine. Each of us is born to be something and I am a firm believer no matter what hobby or interest we have, if we listen we can hear our deepest dreams. It will take us to the pathway to where we need to be, getting signs along the way. These things we find on our path are what we might see as miracles.

As I watched the news and see how many children have been affected by the economy and how many of them are homeless, it breaks my heart. One thing I learned was that they never stopped dreaming and how it doesn't take away the light inside of them.

Some dreams are built on things that happen in our life that shatter lives and unfortunately come from such sadness. However, it still carries a light that shines brighter than any light ever known. It creates a big shift in the world by leaving a huge imprint in the universe. Many people are affected by its bright light, bringing good things to the world and touching many people. Dreaming while sleeping is one thing that I have much experience in because I have been doing it all my life. If you would really like to watch a good movie about dreaming, "Waking Life" is a great in depth thought about dreaming and you may want to watch it more than once because it's very deep, but explains dreaming in a quantum theory way. The graphics are great and it gives the movie a really good natural feel to it.

Like other people, dreams have followed and stayed in my mind throughout my life and I feel that I have been able to understand my dream world. I can go back to sleep and finish a dream and things happen to me in life that brings me back to a dream from long ago. I believe we can travel to any place while dreaming. One dream in particular that really had a big impact on my life was given to me by a friend.

One day while talking with a very close friend about the afterlife, we decided to make a promise to one another. If one of us were to die before the other, we would come back and show each other what it was like in the afterlife. As time went on we continued our life keeping in touch with one another.

Until, the time came and my friend passed away one year to cancer. Never remembering about our promise, years went on as I continued to raise my children. I can tell you that through- out my life around this time, I had many questions about many mystical things in life and this one particular dream took me many years to finish.

I started out on a beach that seemed to be at the end of the world. The sunrise was big with orange and hints of red passed through it horizontally and blended in o the puffy clouds that shattered throughout the sky. It seemed as if I could reach out and touch them. The way the water reflected the sunrise expanded the colors onto the ocean. As I continued to walk following the beach it led me to a large woodland mountain. I began to climb up through the woods and at times I would have to hold on to the trees to push myself up the mountain, so that I could get farther up the hill. Before the dream would end, I would come upon a purple chair or some kind of unusual object, which of course would stick out. So whenever I went back to that dream, I would start where I left off right where the object sat. The objects were always there before and after each dream. This mountain took years to climb and I would have other dreams throughout the years, and never knew when I was going to have the dream again.

On this one particular night in my dream I would make it to the very top of the mountain. The edge was like a wall that was made of earth. I began to feel a mist of fresh air escaping over the edge that chilled the surroundings. I then had to grab a root from a tree that had grown upwards on the earthy wall in order to push myself up, so that I could see the other side. It was like lifting myself over a fence and what was below on the other side was a perfect valley full of nature.

Once over the other side the atmosphere changed and the air I could only describe as being perfect. It was unpolluted and fresh with a very light mist that consumed the air, making dew that settled to the ground causing a white blanket on the earth. As I walked down the hill the dirt below me was the darkest black I had ever seen with gray sparkles in it. When I stepped on it, it reminded me of crumbled dough that squished together. Even though it looked as if it would stick between my toes, it only rolled off without leaving a trace on my feet.

It was a perfect atmosphere of ecosystem that was untouched. In the valley it was full of all different colored trees and plants, but with a very light tint to them. This was due to the mist that was settling around them. There was the sound of a water fall in the back ground and as I began to approach it, I then could see a pond. The water was so clear that if it wasn't for the movement of the water from the waterfall, you would barely see it. Resting comfortably bathing in the water were small birds of all colors and lily pads rested next to white lotus flowers, that were all floating together throughout the pond.

As I continued to walk, I came across some grapes that were growing on a vine and I could not believe my eyes. They were the most perfect grapes I had ever seen before. They were large, husky and had a velvet like color to them with the darkest deep purple. Because of my earthy feelings, I went to reach for one so that I could pluck one off and eat it, but as soon as I did, I could feel someone grabbing my left shoulder and squeezing it. Being very surprised, but not scared I turned and saw my friend there. She was beautiful and wore a very light flowing dress the same color as the fog. She was young somewhere in the middle and I was so glad to see her. She spoke to me telling me that, "We don't do that here." I could see why this place seemed so untouched, because it was a place that just allowed. She told me to stay as long as I wanted. Then turned around and walked the other way disappearing into the fog. I asked her to stay, but she continued to walk leaving me there to wander around. I really don't think time was on my side, because I felt as if I needed to go and time was running short. Although, I have had other strange experiences while dreaming, I have never had one like that before and since. My friend kept her word and I will always love her knowing I will see her again.

In my opinion, dreams are more than just your brain putting together all of these pieces into events that you have in your head. We are with people that have gone to other planes and left us here on earth reaching out to us there. It really does make sense if you look at how we are very relaxed with our body at that time and I believe we enter the spiritual world then.

Some dreams are neurons firing off randomly of all kinds of things in our brain. But, sometimes our dreams are just feelings that we are trying to express from real life, which has been giving us some frustration. It's a tool to help us cope with problems we may be having in life and a way to release our thoughts. The trick is to know the difference when it comes to knowing your dream world. Because we are human beings and our brain is the interpreter and our mind is the generator to produce energy, we have to look at where our dreams are coming from. It's all in your feelings and how you feel about your dreams and what is going on in your life at that moment. Dreams put us into many different situations and help us to dig up our feelings. We can run away from the memory of our problems, but we cannot completely get rid of them until we know it is there. So at times our brain reminds our mind that we are feeling them.

My brain knows that I am dreaming and so I am free to experience the full effects of it. I find that I do not get afraid of my dreams no matter how horrifying it gets, because I simply realize that they will not harm me physically. Many of us say that they do not dream very much or don't dream at all. As soon as we wake up if we don't write them down the memory of them are sometimes lost. So perhaps that's why people feel they don't dream at all. Just waking up to the sound of the alarm clock could distract us and get rid of the memory of our dreams. I love dreaming and look forward to it every time I lay down to sleep. It helps me to connect better with my feelings. Some dreams are from years ago and things that I am doing can trigger them.

Some believe that reality is our nonexistence and our dream life is our real reality. I believe that it's a place to remember our soul and helps us to go home after school lets out. It's a place to express what we go through, throughout our daily lives as human beings. It brings us closer to the ones we love and it helps us to travel anywhere we want. Dreaming is such a good tool to have that helps us to release and remove ourselves from the world. Perhaps we meet living people there and have a soulful experience together.

So what happens when our dreams are filled with scary and hateful thoughts? How do we cope with it? Look at what is going on in your life and maybe you can see the connection. Our minds do intertwine with our dreams and has a funny way of getting its thoughts across to us. Sometimes I get confused about my feelings, wondering why I am having such strange dreams. So I concentrate on the emotion and focus on where I am feeling it in my body. When I can identify where the feeling is coming from then I am able to put the pieces together. At times we humans have a tendency to hide our feelings from ourselves, so I find dreaming to be a good wake up call.

Another thing that I think is a very big distraction when sleeping, doing it while having the television on. Just imagine all of the subliminal messages that you can pick up while sleeping. Especially today with all the strange things that is on in the first place. One thing that I have noticed is how many people do it, because of working night shift at the hospital. Some of the things people listen to during sleep can be very disturbing. I also wonder how it's affecting children during sleep because with all of the meme-tics out there, putting thoughts and suggestions in their minds. Richard Brodie has a great book that explains about memes in our life called "Virus of the Mind." So through allowing ourselves the freedom to open our mind to our dreams and new things in our life helps us to understand ourselves better.

Mind Reflection

I knew I had to be mindful of my surroundings and see the splendor around me. To be thankful for all that was in my life. Just imagine driving the same highway for years, and never really enjoying the magnificent mountain view right in front of you. Now to be mindful is to see the wonderful scenery, which you have been driving by for years and enjoying the splendor of it, as if viewing it for the first time. It may not be what you feel is beautiful, but really it's just that you forgot what you were looking at. Be mindful of your surroundings and see the beauty around you. Remember how it felt to engulf in its newness giving you a feeling of appreciation. The things I view give me a rejuvenating feeling helping my inner spirit. After a while I found that I longed to linger in each emotion and I began to relax more seeing things in a better light.

In a world where we strive to be different, we all seem to want everyone around us to think the same. Help yourself by being grounded and wake in the morning telling yourself, "Today is going to be a good day, no matter what anyone else may think." You will be surprised how instantly you will attract more kindness and happiness around you. I try always to see the beauty around me now, such as a refreshing bed of flowers as I walk by, so smell the roses along the way.

Visualization has so many advantages and is what creates dreams helping with desires. Visualization is also important when doing meditation. Although thinking of nothing is the focus when meditating. It's being able to allow the nothingness, letting go and just being. The best way to work yourself up to this is to visualize yourself in a nice surrounding, letting your thoughts pass by you. This will help you to exercise your ability to focus. There are so many meditation CD's out there that will walk you through the visualization process, painting a picture for you and helping you to flow into a relaxing state. Dr Dyer has a great meditation called "Getting into the Gap." After a while you will begin to be able to use your imagination, while focusing on a mantra.

Mantras are wonderful words, sounds, vibrations, prayers and chants that keeps us focused; helping us to clear our mind of thoughts. Imagine a mantra like a comedian on the stage that has your attention and forgetting everything that is going on in your life at that very moment. Just for that half an hour you focus your attention on the funny humor. This may seem a bit hard for some people and clearing your mind can be a bit of a brain exercise, but not impossible.

Meditation begins with breathing exercises. Let's face it breathing can cause you all types of problems in your body. It affects all parts of the body and this subject alone I have spent years studying. Three good deep breaths in and out, helps to get rid of any tension. So when breathing your three deep breaths; you want to take a nice slow deep breath in through your nose, hold it and exhale slowly through your mouth. After your breathing exercises sit quietly and begin to adjust your body, while making yourself comfortable. Make sure that you are not tense and relax all of your muscles. Begin to clear your mind and adjust you're breathing to be slow, deep, and regular, just feel your breath. You can even see good entering into your body on inhalation and bad going out on exhalation. This makes sense since we breathe in things we need from the earth and exhale waste from our body. Perhaps you can begin to practice this often and look at it as meditation without worry.

It's not as easy as it may sound to just clear your mind or relax. I have heard so many people say that they wish they could meditate and that it wasn't finding the time that was the problem. It's trying to get rid of all those thoughts that keep popping back into their mind. If you are having a hard time clearing your mind, practice visualizing yourself in an empty room painted any color you want. Then feel what it would feel like to be alone in this room. You can practice this when you are with your family. Just close your eyes and feel what it would feel like to be alone in that room at the very moment. Do this by visualizing the room that you have built in your mind. I have this place in my mind, so I can clear my thoughts before meditation. Once I feel that I am alone with my thoughts, I then imagine myself in a glass pyramid box, but you can use any shape you would like. I then begin my mantra and when I have a problem with my thoughts creeping in, I see them outside of the box, and that I am separate from them. I keep focused that I am in the pyramid alone and that I am not a part of my thoughts, because they are separate from me. This helps me with the feeling of being disconnected from them. See it as being in a bus and watching everything through the window as you drive by. So through practice you will get better each time separating your thoughts.

Sometimes you could have good clarity and feel yourself right in the place where you should be. It's the place that feels like pure peace and total relaxation. You feel like you could be there forever with this feeling, but as soon as you think, " Oh I'm in that space," you begin to realize you are out of it. Your thoughts may start to come at you again and the best thing to do is take a couple of deep breaths, starting over again. Just remember, when you get excited about being in that place, just allow it to happen. This may sound funny, but try to not get to excited, so that you will feel yourself allowing.

I was able to use it throughout my life. I would say from as early as I could remember. The word meditation was around me constantly throughout my existence and I learned by watching others. Whenever I am home on my days off I found that how I spent my time was very important, as far as getting the full effects of actually relaxing. I love getting up before dawn and drink some tea, visit my garden and enjoy my dogs: Maggie and Merlin. I like to make it as fun and creative as I can and always love working on some kind of a project.

These special moments will put a smile on your face on those days when you find you are very busy, giving you a feeling of excitement. Just knowing that you will have those moments again will brighten up your day. If you find that you do not have time for these moments in your life, I suggest having one. Give yourself the time in life to discover who you are and you will discover a whole new you.

Meditation can be done in many ways and have such a positive response in your life. There are times when I feel very uptight and can't seem to unwind, so I meditate for a half an hour giving my body a chance to leave this world recharging my battery. People around me have said that they see a difference in me before and after I meditate. I have taken anti-anxiety medication prescribed by my doctor before, for a very short time. The effect of meditation to me is a much better effect. The effects of meditation can outweigh any type of anti-anxiety medication.

Just look at how your body reacts to stress, the way you breathe can cause a chain reaction. You start to increase respiration and that increases your heart rate, in turn increasing your blood pressure, which affect your kidneys and affecting the fluids in your body. So what I have found is during stressful times meditation can keep your blood pressure down. I bought a blood pressure machine and at one point my blood pressure was high, due to the fact that I smoked. I wanted to see if meditation could help me. But, I must say I talked to my doctor about it first and she wanted to keep an eye on it. So I suggest that if you have a problem, please see your doctor.

What I did was take my blood pressure before and after meditation and found that it decreased considerably. Also, finding that if I did it on a daily basis for twenty minutes a day, it kept me very calm all day and I handled things so much better. I wasn't so quick to react. So in my opinion meditation has a greater advantage than when I took anti-anxiety medication for a short period of time. It doesn't have all those bad side effects.

Although many people could find time to meditate, I also have heard many people say that they don't have the time to meditate. There are so many way to meditate that there is no excuse to not do it. It can be a cup of tea in the early morning looking out your window for ten minutes. To me meditation is anything that makes you feel true happiness inside of yourself combined with a sense of relaxation and contentment..

Mindful meditation is a great way to meditate and I find it to be a lot of fun. Those are the times when you enjoy the wonders in your life. I have used mindful meditation from my morning walks, to a beautiful view, to watching the ocean on the beach. If you have never really gotten in the habit of meditation there are so many different kinds to choose from to fit any life style. Start out slow and read up on it. Look at all the options, tools and classes around you. There is so much media out there that one can learn in the comfort of their home.

When my children were small I would do my meditation while lying in bed right before sleeping. I had bought some sound tracks of some good teachers that would paint a surrounding for me, helping me to mediate. With raising two children, being a wife, student and working as a waitress, it would help me to have a very restful sleep, feeling rejuvenated in the morning.

Now that I am older as well as my children grown, I have had time in my life to pick any time to meditate. I love playing soothing music all the time in my home and found that cable TV and the internet has some good options. Many of you may know about the chakras, and I would like to go over them, because I would like to share an exercise that I do to help me understand my feelings. Through meditation I have been able to work with the energy that I produce in my body. What made up of a person's aura are the seven chakras. Chakras are spinning energy that has a color and is located on a certain part of the body. There are seven of them and are associated with a color and a musical note creating a certain vibration.

At the base of the spine is the color red. It is associated with the musical note C and it helps us to feel grounded. Next, is located below the naval in the sacral area and is the color orange associated with the musical note D. Its meaning is associated with intimacy. The chakra located at the solar plexus and is the color yellow, has a musical note of E and is associated with our_emotions, creativity, as well as knowledge. Now my favorite and located at the heart and associated with it is the color green with the musical note of F and of course its meaning is love. The chakra located at the throat is blue; it's for communication and has the musical note of G. Also, the charka located between the eyes brows is purple and its note is A. It helps with the third eye. Finally, the chakra located at the crown of the head is violet, its musical note is B and it helps us with the divine.

Now with each chakra there is a feeling that we can feel inside of us. For instance, when we fall in love or have love for something, it opens up our heart chakra, helping us to project love to the outside world. So how I have been able to use this in meditation is what I like to call point the finger. Point the finger tells me where it is that I am feeling a certain emotion, so that I can find where it is coming from.

I sit and think about it feeling the emotion and situation that I may be in and find where it is that I am feeling these emotions. Then I can point the finger were I am having this hidden emotion. Try it next time you are confused about a certain emotion. There are some good books that really explain the chakras in detail and authors have written a whole book on the subject alone.

Just like Louise Hay's book, "You Can Heal Your Life," believes that our feelings have everything to do with our health and how many diseases are associated with emotions. Check out her movie, "You Can Heal Your Life," by streaming it on Hay House.

Therefore, meditation can be one of the best things that you could do for yourself. If you are interested in starting your new adventure learning about meditation, start your research and you will find the right meditation for your life.

Core of Self Image

For the longest time I never knew what an ego was until I read the book "Be Here Now," by Ram Dass, that helped me to understand what an ego really was. I had the privilege to have a heart to heart talk with Ram Dass, through web cam, from his home in Hawaii, to my home in Florida. He was able to answer my questions that I had about ego and learned so much through our conversation. I found out that when I let go of ego, I felt close to my soul, helping me to see others soul.

Ego is like a nagging itch you cannot seem to get rid of and it can be everywhere. The first thing I did was recognize what ego was in a daily life, so that I could be conscious of it. I wanted to stay away from it, giving me a great feeling of contentment. The more I say no to my ego, the more I instantly feel a relief from stress. I began to see the good side to it; for once I was not so concerned about what others thought of me. I found that people accepted me for who I am, instead of what they wanted me to be. I was truthful to myself, knowing that I was not perfect and at times I would trip over my ego. When I was aware of it, I was able to stay true to my path and get directions by looking for signs along the way. Ego comes in all forms and it doesn't always have to involve money. When you begin to see how it works and become more conscious of it, then you will begin to see your own ego, and how it gets in the way of who you truly want to be. There is this game I call ego pong and I am sure everyone has seen it. It's where a conversation is based on two or more people, trying to outdo each other with their ego. It could seem like a common conversation that is mistaken for just a nice chat. Next time you are around a group of people be aware of it, by just sitting back and watching how each one of us use ego. This means including yourself and whenever I got sucked into it, I felt a bit silly. So being aware of it helps you to become closer to your true-self.

Be happy for others when something good happens in their life without resentment or wanting what they have. When you can really feel happiness for others, it comes back to you with the love and happiness you enjoy in life. Something happens when you feel truly happy for others, you begin to feel their happiness, and it becomes a shared moment.

To be who you were born to be should start with letting go of the ego. This frees up time, so that you can accomplish things without, what I call mind chatter. Mind chatter is that ugly ego talking in the back ground, changing your choices throughout your day. To be jealous of someone is egos way of making us feel, as if we are not good enough. Also to want others to be jealous of us is egos way of making us feel, as if we need approval. Like Ram Dass say, "When we are aware of our ego, it brings us closer to soul and this helps us to see others as a soul."

To feel guilty for what you may have in life is not good, to appreciate what you have in life is what surrounds you with much happiness. When you are thankful for what you have and appreciate the things you have accomplished, the universe hears you. To look for lack in your life only leaves you with more of it, but if you are thankful for everything that is in your life, the universe will help you grow in good ways. See the universe as supportive instead of non-supportive. Even if others may think you are without, do not let their egos and yours keep you from allowing good things in your life.

What I found was that when I released the feeling of what others thought of me, I was able to reach for better things in my life. I found that I was not living someone else's life, living the way others wanted. What about when others feel as if they are better than others? I really cannot think of anyone who likes to be treated as if they are less than others. The ego likes people to feel as if they are better than others, because it's the egos way of keeping us separate from one another. I believe that if we felt safe with ourselves then we would be able to understand that. Since I have learned much about ego, I have learned a lot about the soul as well.

This sounds a bit funny to me now because the soul lives within me, but I was very confused about the soul and what it meant to me in my life. Like the ego I really only had a small bit of knowledge about it and wondered what soul was in a more in depth meaning. Soul is what makes you who you are in the universe, it's part of everything and anything and is connected to all. It's what connects you to God, Higher Power etc. It's the reason why you are born to be who you were meant to be. It's you, it's the part of you that felt the joy when you were very little. Its peace and joy and what makes us whole. If ones soul shifts it never leaves another untouched. We shift together in life because we are living energy that affects each other. We fool ourselves in life and separate ourselves from one another, thinking that others will not affect us, but in reality everything affects us. How could it not? When you meet someone and begin to see their soul you become good friends or may become lovers, but something clicked or triggered you in a good way and you connected to their soul. This opens your heart giving you much love for that person. To see the child in others can connect you to their soul.

It's the part that makes you feel connected to how you felt as a child. It can be felt on those nights when you are alone and no one is there to judge you. That's why spending time alone is good for everyone. It's what connects us to the truth and has endless. But we have put on blinders sometimes in life by not understanding others, but if we lifted the blinder we could see we are all the same. Try this the next time you see someone you feel you have absolutely no connection to, by visualizing them as a child. Perhaps you can do what I do with patients and see them as someone you know. You will find that something changes in you and you begin to feel empathy. When you feel empathy for someone, it's the souls way of saying it's near. It's not hard to recognize the soul, because it has been with you since the beginning.

Why we have a hard time knowing the difference between the soul and personality is because we have spent a lifetime being wired, placing thoughts in our brains, associating them with feelings and the right way to feel. The soul doesn't need to know anything about the material world and can easily be seen as a pure thought. It's the innocence we had before we began to judge something or someone.

Soul is what makes miracles and when connected to it can uplift one. The universe is like a big ball of energy, with many colors blended together as if on a painter's canvas. To change one part of it would change the whole pattern. We share that energy and as a child I can remember how strong

I felt it in my innocent mind. We can be whatever we want to be and we can create what we want in our life, but first it must be who we truly are. It sounds so easy, but we could question it our whole life.

The soul sees no color and is able to connect to others, feeling it to the core. It is such a blessing that I am able to remember my childhood at such an early age, because I believe that it's there where we are the closest to the purity of our soul. When I was a child I would stare at myself in the mirror until I could feel a disconnection from my body. With all of the energy out in the universe, surely the energy I have lives on. Check out the movie Quantum Activist and get a good explanation of his ideas.

One morning when I woke, I felt very sad and could not understand this, because everything was going so well in my life. In fact this was a better day than any other day. It was my weekly dinner with my husband and loving adult children. So, why was I so depressed? Why did I have a feeling as if my world was falling down around me? I had to really look at this for a bit before it got out of hand and ruined my whole day.

So, why was I trying to go backwards? Why? Why? Why? This is all I could say to myself. This was the silliest thing. Why would someone be ready to have a wonderful day and feel like all is doomed? I realized that I felt very unsafe within myself. I began to tell myself, "I am safe," "I am safe," "I am safe. "As I began to tell myself this many times repeating it to myself over and over again. I wanted to feel as if today was a new day. I really could feel the love around me and how today was a safe day. If I had to tell myself that every day I was going to do just that.

By telling myself that I was safe I noticed slowly how I started to feel much better. I came to the conclusion that I really didn't want to know how it got there anymore. All I knew was that somehow I picked up this bad habit from something that happened to me. I was tired at this point in my life of analyzing it. All I knew was its there and the simplest thing to do was to see how safe I was right at this very moment.

I believe that when we are children, we are very fragile as far as being wired in our thoughts. Simply put, this is not a perfect world. There is negativity in this world and most of us have things in our mind as children that have shocked us in some form or another. Look, when you come from a divine place to life, it has its moments. Let's face it, we even have those moments as adults.

Sometimes in our life we have things that happen that are unspeakable. You then see that the world is not so happy. You're so used to watching your back; you truly do not relax fully. So to get rid of that keep telling yourself that you are safe now in life. Besides feeling safe in the world, I wanted to learn to slow down a bit. We do live in a world that is a fast paced motor race. We feel the changes that the earth has and how it's affecting us to become speed maniacs. We really need to understand that it's very important for us to have time for each other.

Sometimes we feel we must have a goal in order to feel as if we are accomplishing something. We begin to feel as if we are unsettled in life, as if we cannot see what we have accomplished. We want to achieve goals in life because it gives us a feeling of excitement and achievement. If having a goal gives you the best feeling ever, then I say, have a goal. But, many of us feel empty even if we have a goal, as if this is not good enough. You may feel you are just so unhappy with yourself, because you simply cannot see the great things you have done so far.

Then I say get rid of the goals and have hobbies. Start that yoga classes you always wanted to do, or do something that brings much interest to you. If going back to school is who you are and you enjoy it to its fullest, by all means go for it. I think everyone should have hobbies, because these are the things that connect us to ourselves. I believe in enjoying your life and surrounding yourself with the interests that you like.

All I am saying is if you are doing something in your life in order to please others or the ego and it's not working for you, then in my opinion, maybe you should look for that hobby. I can remember when I decided that I wanted to learn more about myself. I was asked once by a counselor in my early teens a series of questions about myself. What's your favorite color? What's your favorite pie? After about the tenth question, I learned that I knew nothing about myself. So from that day forward I swore that I needed to slow down in life and get to know more about myself.

Time really does heal us from pain, because of our need to be happy. Such pain in our lives, we will always remember. Unless there is a magic way of wiping it out, we will always remember pain in our life, but it's how we handle and see that pain. The pain we have endured, we lived through. Some of us escaped barely and when the survival techniques were no longer needed, it hard wired us to keep it for safe keeping. So what do we do when pain has been so unbearable that we feel as if we cannot go on any longer? We reach for a living soul and take love by its hand. We learn to trust again, getting rid of the need to punish someone else for our pain creating more.

Children suffer much pain in life because of adults who feel they have the right to be a victim. Not looking at the way things have changed in their life and the responsibility they now have. We do not want to become that abuser and breaking the cycle is very important to do in life, so that all can heal around you. Sometimes the pain is so unbearable that we hide it and don't recognize it for what it is. We deny that pain and it comes out in other ways. To make peace and move on is one thing, but to ignore it trying to move on is another. We really need to make peace with it, so that triggers and bad thoughts do not cloud our minds.

Dear Abusers

Through the two years of self-change I can truly say that I have made peace with myself. This is to you wherever you are.

Dear John Doe,

    I am sure you are wondering why I am writing you. So to help your curiosity, here I go. . Because of you I help others. Because of you I have become a strong, loving and caring human being. Because of you I have been able to have a loving family and able to have empathy for others. I no longer have any hatred for you. You are free from the anger I have had towards you and I no longer wish you harm nor do I want you to suffer, but I hope that you will be able to make peace within yourself. I pray for you to have much healing in your life. Much light in your life, Donna.

    I realized that I had control over how I viewed my abusers,. I was able to change the way I thought by just changing bad thoughts into better ones. After a while I was able to do it automatically and begin to feel the moment. I found myself feeling more like myself, after all these years. I connected to my soul and rejected ego and found a spiritual experience. I have learned to love more than I have ever before, appreciate love much more than I have ever done before. I connect to that childlike love and it increases my endorphins. To know that I can grab the moment anytime I want, really has been the best gift of all.

    You may be wondering about all the dirty details of my abuse, but in reality it's over in my life, it no longer exists Plus there are too many people involved and I don't want to hurt the ones I love, and that includes the abusers.

Look, it doesn't matter if you live under a bridge, hop trains to travel, live a large luxury life, a celebrity, rock star, teacher, police officer, doctor, nurse, respiratory therapist, or any other life people live in this world. All that matter is happiness and love is among you, so that you can radiate love as we pass one another throughout life. Pain may seem like a horrible way to live, it doesn't have to really exist, but it does. We look at all of the people and things that are going on now in life and we tell ourselves; it's useless. There are too many people and too much going on that there is no way everyone will ever be on the same level, plane, or channel. Perhaps your right, perhaps this is really how it's always going to be for us, or perhaps things will eventually level out and we will all live in peace. I don't know to tell you the truth, but one thing that I do know is this is now and I choose love. So perhaps you will choose love on your journey. This will only increase the vibration in life, bringing peace to you allowing its light to enter your world and direct you to your soul.

As I went through this journey, I could see how all it took was just reaching out and allowing. Do not get sucked into the mundane things in life, just understand it, allow it and move on. Oh! And don't worry about all that nonsense that has already passed. Allow yourself to heal and you will learn so much making you strong like bull. So remember your soul is really you and don't forget it.

For the first time I am allowing in my life, and what comes next I really don't know. But, what I do know is that I will never look back anymore on the bad things in my life. It was only the memories that kept them alive. I cannot express how much my life has changed. Even though I have others things in my life to learn, I feel this has helped to clear the path, so that I can walk through the rest of my journey a bit easier. If I learned anything throughout this journey is that it's a continual lesson here on earth. So this is just the beginning of another chapter. I can tell you one thing; I will be able to handle it much better in my life. No longer do I feel a heaviness on my head and although there is more to come. It's about feeling safe with me, spreading love, and sharing myself with the ones who I connect with in this life. I find it to be exciting to be a part of this world and relating to others. It allowed the wall that has been up to come crashing down without any resistance, freedom from an unwanted memory that happened way back when. Be on your own personal journey to find yourself. Really make some serious changes in your life. Share what it is to be a part of this world in a loving and caring way. The instant you believe a thought it has no choice but to go into existence.

Take things day by day using techniques I used in this book, or make your own list of things you feel that need to be addressed in your life. By working on each one you will begin to see how they all connect to one another. How each one leads to the next change in your life. There are so many tools out there that can help you on your journey. Take a chance and live your true wishes. Be that person, imagine yourself doing these things, feeling as if you are there. You deserve nothing but the truth. By looking at what is keeping you locked into the mode, feeling stuck, it's as simple as reaching into your pocket and taking out the key.

Pressure of being something that you are not, keeps you from living the lifestyle that you want. Take pleasure in your lifestyle don't worry about what others may assume about how you are living it. Live it the way you desire, as long as you are not hurting yourself or others then you are working with love. It has its advantages because there is much growth and moving ahead. Then your real self will continue to grow and flourish. You are the only one who lives with your mind and knows your soul.

Mommy

To this day I love my mother to pieces. She was the breast that I laid my head on as a baby, and her heart beat was the first thing I heard as I laid in her belly. She was given to me, to help me to advance my soul. Many times I would listen to her with her friends, as she advised them when every they came to her with their problems, which was often. I was mesmerized by how she spoke, carefully watching her help another human being.

My mother has become a very strong human being and has such a wonderful soul. She has helped me to be who I am today, by simply giving me what was needed for me to advance my soul. I cannot even imagine what life would have been like if she would of refused to hear her calling. Her choices helped me to get the right lessons as I grew stronger in life.

Although I have always seen my mother as a strong human being, she too was once a child just like me. To this day my mother is living a nice retirement as an individual and enjoying living in the now. Once a little young flower child hippie from the sixties, she has settled down in life enjoying family. I know that she struggles at times with days that no longer exist and I say to her now, "You are a beautiful human being and always have been." I have pleasant memories with her and when I am around certain sounds and smells, such as the taste of cold eggplant parmesan; as we ate together on the couch in the living room one night. To those nights talking to her at the foot of her bed, I will cherish those days forever. I love you mommy.

Our Love

To this day Rich is my best friend and like all relationships we by far have had our share of disagreements. It may have looked at times to others as if it was not a perfect relationship, but to us it could not have been any more perfect. We have been teaching and learning from one another since our twenties and he has watched me go through my troubles loving me through them all.

To the day we stood before God and announced our love, to that day he got into the shower with all his clothes on with me and held me, telling me that I was a good person, as I cried my heart out. Makes me so proud to be his wife, because even on those days I felt as if no one loved me, he made me feel special and loved. I will always love him for that.

We have learned so much about one another and just like my children, I have felt he too was with me in many lives. Our birthdays are one day apart from one another; which connects us together even more. One thing I can say for sure, we never forget each other's birthdays. I have been so blessed to have found him.

Relationships can be a bit challenging and many are not up for the challenges it brings. We had our troubles I admit, but we were able to reach out and always fix it. Now that we have some history together and have turned into so many different people since we met. We know that if we go through anymore bumps in the future; we will be masters at repairing them. There were times we both could of bit the head off of a snake, because we butted our heads together. Like I said it's not a perfect relationship maybe in someone else world, but it's perfect for us.

If you think someone's life, such as a sibling's relationship is wrong for them; first ask one question. Is anyone getting hurt? If not then just because your brother-law farts in public or his ego is bigger than Texas, I say love your dear ones decision. Really, do you have enough time to even worry about it? It only puts a strain on you and your dear one's lives. Enjoy your loved one's no matter what they choose. You can only love them through it by allowing and helping. These are the things that will help them the most. But, just remember your loved ones may not like the way your spouse burps at the table, or how his butt crack hangs out when he bends over We all have something that just may be very strange to a lot of people, neither of us are better than the other. So I say concentrate on loving one another instead of finding fault. It's just egos way of wanting us to stir the pot, confusing one another.

You are Loved

Throughout my life I have always seemed to search for love from others. I believe the more I searched and wanted, the more the universe gave me a continual search and want feeling. In fact if you just give love and expect nothing back, it will bring more love your way. Love seems to be a big mystery to many people and how we think about love. We question love a lot when really it shouldn't even require questioning.

Sometimes we worry about being hated instead of seeing how much we are loved. Love should not be complicated, but because of a lot of past things that happen to us, we use many different ways to stay clear of being hurt again and this just keeps us very lonely and angry. It's important that we find the love of ourselves first. Hate requires a lot of energy on our part, but love requires a great deal of nothing. It requires no work and uses less energy on our part. Because when we love, we are allowing. It just exists and with love comes all the things that are good.

When Rich came home from work to tell me the factory that was open for forty years was going to be shut down in three months, I remained calm and told him, "Congratulations now you can move on" I had learned that from a lecture from Dr. Wayne Dyer I had watched on PBS. So Rich took a leap of faith and began school. Something he had always wanted to do and felt that it was a huge challenge, not seeing the potential in the beginning. It was something that he gently slid into, adapting very well.

Although he eventually relaxed into school it took time to get there and patience was one thing I definitely had trouble with most of my life. It created such anxiety that it left me with a feeling of being unsettled. Also we had a routine that was being broken and our way of being settled into one another was being totally disrupted.

Because I was going through a shift in my life I was not realizing Richard was going through his own shift in his life. It was a major quantum shift in our life together as well. But, there was a time when we began to clash very badly. So we got tired of fighting it and fighting one another that we realized what was really going on with our life. We learned we were going through a shift in our life for a reason. So I had to learn patients and I practice the art of living in the now.

It's funny how we think that once we settle into a way of life and grow that it will be the only one we go through. Just like now in my life it would be silly for me to think that this is the last of my changes.

I have always built my life around my children and it was about time that I made some changes in my life, as an individual entering the world. Because I had them at such an early time in my life, for the first time in my life I will be stepping out into the world as an individual. I know now in my life that I cannot go on in this world not doing what I have dreamt about and I would rather die than to just settle in my life because of fear. We change by moving forward and like it or not we are moving forward to disappear in the vacuum of the afterlife. I plan on making the most of my life and if that means giving up things that I have attached myself to then so be it. We are so consumed in material things in the world that we get emotionally attached to them. As if they can speak to us and love us through our troubles. But in the end you will be left with only yourself and the memories of loved ones near you on your death bed.

Everything you thought that was going to stay the same never does in the world. I gave up things in my life that I thought would be around forever and decided I wasn't going to settle for attaching myself to some material item. I also learned that I welcomed prosperity and stopped feeling guilty for having it and to appreciate what I do have in life. Although it may look different to some people as if I were poor.

I have seen many people stay in situations that only hold them back. Perhaps it's a job and you stay because you're working for a future goal. That's fine as long as you are content and happy, while doing other things that fulfill your life. But, if you are just down right miserable and hate every waking day just knowing you have to go to that wicked place yet another day, I say get out and run as fast as you can and never look back. That will only leave you to be sick emotionally and eventually physically. We can change the things we don't like by finding other things around us.

I had a wonderful friend that passed away after thirty years of a job he despised. His big dream was to buy lots of land and he saved all of his personal leave time and planned on cashing it in, to help pay for the land. As soon as he retired and ready for his dream he passed away. Two thousand hours he could of taken to enjoy his life and live much happier. I'm not saying don't save for the future, I'm just saying fulfill your life today, by reaching for something that will make you happy. Dreams are not based on hurting others intentionally just to get to where you want to go. Dreams are based on a good feeling.

Once I had been able to remove all of the things in my life that were not good for me and understood where they were coming from, I was able to see that everything in my life prepared me for this moment today. Also once I was able to understand, I was able to relax more into myself and this gives me contentment in my life.

I went through many changes and it was like a carnival ride with unexpected things popping out at me, as I trusted the trolley to drive through the path. I must say there were surprises quite often and although there were stressful days, by the next day I was able to work through them seeing the world in a better light. I am after all human and I still may get my feathers ruffled from time to time, but I handle it much better not allowing it to stay with me.

Most of all I have learned to not live my life in fear and that in order to make things happen, I had to step outside of my box and conquer it. I knew that if I lived my life in fear, that my life would not grow the way I wanted it to. Think of yourself like a flower and how you have to reach for the light in order to grow. Although change is something we go through all the time, I had a problem as a young adult getting adjusted to it. It took me a long time to do so, but I was never one to settle, and believe without growth I would not be as happy in life.

Be who you were born to be is about living your dreams and allowing it to take form. To understand who you are and how your path has brought you to where you are today, using it as a tool. To remove all of the things in life that you were taught that didn't fit you and wasn't who you were.

Instead of being so hard on yourself, for not being who others want you to be. It was just a square peg in a round hole and all you have to do is just simply get the right peg for the right hole. It's okay to dream outside of your box, even when you may be looked at as silly to others, or criticized for that round peg that fits so well in your life. Just remember that if it fits you it's who you are.

It's about looking at your lessons from the past that may have left a scare, as a tool to be who you are now in life. This will help you to allow yourself to let go and invite others into your world. Once you have realized who you truly are and begin to dream, you will light the spark that will begin that flame inside of you. It will carry you through a new exciting journey through life. You will begin to see how all the pieces begin to fit together around you, leading you to many adventures on your path, allowing you to be who you were born to be.

Exercises for Change

I have put together these exercises I used during my journey of self-change. Give yourself time with each exercise, so that you can get the most out of each one. Be open to the experience and allow it. This will help you to build willpower and become strong like bull! You can do these in any order.

One: See the truth about yourself and situations around you. See what it is that needs changing in your life that will bring happiness to you. Be honest with yourself and remember that you hold the key to your happiness. Look at how you have handled them up until now. Give yourself time with this and observe it. Do not be hard on yourself during this process but be honest. Imagine daily yourself with that change in your life. Fantasize about it like you did when you were a child. Try doing it when you have time alone and hold it in the back of your mind throughout your daily life.

Two: Triggers can be a part of our habits and actions. Like my life, I felt like certain things just bothered me and I could not really explain why. Once you have been able to relax into changing into what it is that you want in your life, you will begin to see the things that trigger you. Study the elements that seem to trigger these things in your life and change those triggers by replacing them with a more positive choice, or actions. This will help you to form better habits and help rewire your brain to better thoughts.

Three: Many times we look to the one who has caused us pain waiting for them to apologize or an explanation as to why this happened. As if we are waiting to heal ourselves giving them power over us. This gives us a sense of denial and frustration in our life. We are in denial because we do not want to believe that we are the ones keeping these thoughts in our life and keeping our abuse alive, causing us to become a victim. Begin to see what it is that causes you to hold on to your past situations. If its anger, start to understand that your anger is hurt. Begin to let yourself feel that hurt and plan some days to be alone by having a retreat for yourself, using this time to comfort yourself and have plenty of tissues at hand.

Four: Start creating good memories to replace the bad ones. Be with the ones you love in life. Do things that help you to connect to a loving atmosphere. Hold on to the good memories as a child and replace your past bad memories with new ones.

Five: We all have ego and I myself seemed to be a bit confused as to what ego was. Start making decisions that do not include your ego. Start listening to others talk and try to recognize it. Learn to love your ego by feeling sorry for it. This will help you to understand it.

Six: Begin to look around you and see the world as a safe place, telling yourself that you are safe. Research a way that you can get some meditation time in on a daily basis. Begin to see the world around you in a much more calmer atmosphere and begin your day with more positive thoughts. Let your wall down and begin to open yourself up to allowing new experiences by trusting your happiness. You may have felt because of the past that every time something good happens to you in your life, that something bad is going to happen too, looking at it as if it were bad luck. Try to allow yourself to enjoy the moment and reject and refuse to think bad thoughts that are entering your mind. Also remember how you felt as a child when you were very happy. Use all of your senses to remind you of all of these feelings.

Seven: Do not limit your dreams and start reaching outside of your box and comfort zone by rejecting fear. If you have lived a life of feeling unsettled and fear has kept you from doing the things in life that will bring much happiness, change it. Try taking baby steps in order to get you much more comfortable about leaving your comfort zone. Look for little messages along the way telling you that you are on the right path. By doing this you will find that you will attract a new path that will lead you to your dreams. Think what you are.

Eight: Begin to see yourself as a loving human being and let yourself begin to see that everything you have gone through in the past is who you have become up until now. See all the good qualities in yourself and appreciate your life. Feel that you deserve to be happy and use mindful meditation throughout your day. Use all your senses to trigger good thoughts. Think of exciting things that are going on around you in your life today, by focusing more on the positive things than the negative. Relish in the fact knowing that you are old enough to have a peaceful life because you hold the power to live the life you desire.

Nine: Learn to accept change in your life. Let go of things that you have an attachment to that no longer serve its purpose and that is getting in the way of you r growth. Also, to allow the flow of life to take place and enjoy living in the moment. Start to appreciate prosperity in you r life while being humble and caring for others. Try to not create resistance in your life by trying to control others around you or belittling someone who is on a different level than you. Simply love them and be there for them. Live in the now and reject thinking of the past and future. Even though you have dreams look at them as if you are living them now and don't worry about the future, because if you can feel yourself living it now, you can begin to see it in the present. Use the words I am instead of I'm going to and just be instead of becoming. You deserve to be happy!

Please visit my blog: http://www.breathofchild.blog.com

Arntz, William, Chasse Betsy, & Vincente Mark (2007) What the Bleep do We Know: (TM): Discovering the endless possibilities for altering your everyday reality. Florida, Deerfield Beach: Health Communications Inc.

Brodie, Richard (2011) Virus of The Mind: The new science of the meme. California, Carlsbad: Hay House Inc.

Dass, Ram (1971) Be Here Now: Cook book for a sacred life. New Mexico, San Cristobal: The Crown Publishing Group, New York New York

Dyer, Wayne (2011) Excuses Begone: How to change a self-defeating thinking habits. California, Carlsbad: Hay House Inc.

Dyer, Wayne (2002) Getting in The Gap: Edition unstated edition. California, Carlsbad: Hay House Inc

Hay, Lousie L. (1999) You Can Heal Your Life: The text of this book is based on You Can Heal Your Life @ 1984,1987.California, Carlsbad: Hay House Inc.

Lost In Space, Deadliest Of Species: Don Richardson 1967

Quantum Activist:Dir. Ri Stewart, Renee Slade 2009.

Waking Life. Dir. Bob Sabiston, Richard Linklater 2002.

You Can Heal Your Life. Michael Goorjain 2007.

www.ingramcontent.com/pod-product-compliance
Lightning Source LLC
Chambersburg PA
CBHW030401290526
45785CB00004B/1857